Bloom's

GUIDES

E. L. Doctorow's
Ragtime

CURRENTLY AVAILABLE

1984
All the Pretty Horses
Beloved
Brave New World
The Crucible
Cry, the Beloved Country
Death of a Salesman
Hamlet
The Handmaid's Tale
The House on Mango Street
I Know Why the Caged Bird Sings
Lord of the Flies
Macbeth
Maggie: A Girl of the Streets
Ragtime
The Scarlet Letter
Snow Falling on Cedars
To Kill a Mockingbird

Bloom's
GUIDES

E.L. Doctorow's
Ragtime

Edited & with an Introduction
by Harold Bloom

CHELSEA HOUSE
P U B L I S H E R S
A Haights Cross Communications ✦ Company
P h i l a d e l p h i a

© 2004 by Chelsea House Publishers, a subsidiary of Haights Cross Communications.

A Haights Cross Communications ⭡ Company

Introduction © 2004 by Harold Bloom.

Printed and bound in the United States of America.

First Printing
1 3 5 7 9 8 6 4 2

Library of Congress Cataloging-in-Publication Data

E.L. Doctorow's *Ragtime* / edited and with an introduction by Harold Bloom.
    p. cm. — (Bloom's guides)
Includes bibliographical references and index.
  ISBN 0-7910-7880-9
  1. Doctorow, E. L., 1931- Ragtime. 2. New York (State)—In literature.
I. Bloom, Harold. II. Series. PS3554.O3R34 2004 813'.54—dc22
                        2003025906

Chelsea House Publishers
1974 Sproul Road, Suite 400
Broomall, PA 19008-0914

www.chelseahouse.com

Contributing editor: Pamela Loos
Cover design by Takeshi Takahashi
Layout by EJB Publishing Services

Contents

Introduction

HAROLD BLOOM

Ragtime, while a charming romance to reread twenty-five years after publication, is far from being Doctorow's most eminent work. That seems to me the recent, highly experimental and poignant *City of God*, a superb phantasmagoria whose inmost concern is the Holocaust. Of Doctorow's earlier fictions, *The Book of Daniel* and *The Waterworks* linger on in my consciousness, as *Ragtime* will not. And yet *Ragtime* is not only Doctorow's greatly deserved popular success: it is a subtle inversion of the formulas that help engender all those period pieces we keep mistaking for permanent achievements, from *The Old Man and the Sea* through *Beloved*. By deliberately composing *Ragtime* as a period piece of 1916, covering the decade previous, Doctorow armors his entertainment against time's revenges. Jonathan Raban, in a formidable critique, found *Ragtime* to be more fragile than cunning, and yet the fragility is itself slyly deliberate.

Ragtime, like much of Doctorow, is a romance rather than a novel. I mean by this an authentic genre difference, since "romance" is now a debased term in our usage, meaning little more than a bodice-ripper. The romance, perfected in English by Sir Walter Scott, Hawthorne, the Brontës, and William Morris, is a narrative fiction in which psychological characterization is replaced by a concern with figurative types, states-of-being, visionary places, and fantastic transformations. Doctorow's *City of God* is his romance culmination, but only *The Book of Daniel* seems to me more novel than romance.

Coalhouse Walker, of the invented personalities in *Ragtime*, is at once the most interesting and the most derivative, since he is a version of Kleist's great story of injustice and violence, "Michael Kohlhaas." As a realistic representation, Walker would be absurd, but the huge irony and stylistic indirection of Doctorow's narrative make the jazz pianist-turned-rebel persuasive: Coalhouse Walker was never harsh or autocratic.

He treated his followers with courtesy and only asked if they thought something ought to be done. He dealt with them out of his constant sorrow. His controlled rage affected them like the force of a magnet. He wanted no music in the basement quarters. No instrument of any kind. They embraced every discipline. They had brought in several cots and laid out a barracks. They shared kitchen chores and housecleaning chores. They believed they were going to die in a spectacular manner. This belief produced in them a dramatic, exalted self-awareness.

The repetitions and reductive simplicity are cultic and ideological, and as such a little disquieting, since I could imagine substituting "Timothy McVeigh" for "Coalhouse Walker" in this passage, with each of the followers a Terry Nichols. Critics who complained that *Ragtime* was a Leftist allegory missed the point: Doctorow is not Jack London, and the comic-strip elements in *Ragtime* imply throughout that any political allegory is easily reversible.

You can say against *Ragtime*, when you stand back from it, that it is already the book of the epic musical it became. There is also the inevitable peculiarity that the historical personages are more exuberant and successful representations than Doctorow's invented figures: Emma Goldman has some force and substance, the revolutionary Younger Brother remains an abstraction. Yet Doctorow, well aware of this, takes every advantage of it. Coalhouse Walker and Younger Brother are not invested with any pathos or resonance; Harry Houdini is, and yet the investment is itself another controlled irony.

When I read *Ragtime* in 1975, its deliberate thinness or fragility bothered me, now, rather less so. With George W. Bush as President, we are back in 1906 again, or at least we will get there if the current government is able to pass and implement its program. The age of J. P. Morgan has come again, but this time to an on-line America. Our current farce is prophesied by *Ragtime*, and Doctorow's insights into our country's nature and history are all-too-likely to be sustained in the years ahead.

Biographical Sketch

Edgar Lawrence Doctorow was born on January 6, 1931 to David R. and Rose Lenin Doctorow in New York City. He graduated from the Bronx High School of Science and attended Kenyon College in Gambier, Ohio, where he received a philosophy degree in 1952. Doctorow studied drama in the graduate department at Columbia University from 1952-1953, and then served in the U.S. Army from 1953–1955. He married Helen Seltser in 1954, and they eventually had three children together. Doctorow worked as a reservations clerk at LaGuardia Airport for a time, and then moved on to read scripts for CBS Television and Columbia Picture Industries. In 1959, Doctorow became the senior editor for New American Library and worked there until 1964, when he became editor-in-chief for Dial Press.

Doctorow had published his first novel, *Welcome to Hard Times*, in 1960. He continued to write, delving into science fiction with *Big as Life*—a futuristic satire set in New York City—published in 1966. In 1969, Doctorow left Dial Press to focus on his writing career and became writer-in-residence at the University of California, Irvine. Doctorow published *The Book of Daniel* in 1971, which was nominated for the National Book Award and established his reputation.

From 1971–1978 Doctorow taught at Sarah Lawrence College in Bronxville, New York. During this time he published *Ragtime*, arguably the defining novel of his career, in 1975. *Ragtime* received the National Book Critics Circle Award for fiction and the American Academy and National Institute of Arts and Letters Award. In 1978, his play, *Drinks for Dinner*, was produced off-Broadway at the Public Theatre. Doctorow continued to write prolifically in the 1980s and 1990s, publishing *Loon Lake* (1980), *Lives of the Poets; Six Stories and a Novella* (1984), *World's Fair*, which received the American Book Award in 1986, *Billy Bathgate* in 1989, which received the National Book Critics Circle Award and the Pen Faulkner Award, and *The Waterworks* (1994). He also published *Scenes and Sequences* with Eric Fischl in 1989 and *Poets and Presidents*, a collection of essays in 1993. Doctorow published *City of God* in 2000, an ambitious novel that experiments with literary technique and examines the great mysteries of human existence.

Over his career Doctorow has also held teaching positions at Princeton University and Yale University Drama School. He has received honorary degrees from Brandeis University and Hobart and William Smith College. He is currently the Lewis and Loretta Glucksman Professor in American Letters of English at New York University.

The Story Behind the Story

When E.L. Doctorow published his fourth book, *Ragtime*, in 1975, it solidified his writing career, and to this day it may still be his most popular work. The book received great praise, yet within just six months of publication, a storm of negative criticism ensued. With most of the negative criticism subsiding over time, the book probably remains Doctorow's most analyzed work.

Ragtime drew attention as a historical novel and was categorized with the works of such authors as Thackeray, Tolstoy, Barth, and Mailer. At the same time, though, the book was different than those produced by such authors. In nineteenth-century historical novels, historical events stand in the foreground; and in twentieth-century historical novels, the historical events serve as background for individuals. But in Doctorow's work, historical and fictional events at times merge, and historical people freely interact with each other as well as with fictional characters.

As a result of Doctorow's mixing of historical persons with created fictional characters, some critics focused on questioning fact versus fiction in the book. Many who found fault with the book were disturbed that history seemingly should be made light of within a work of fiction. "In response to renewed questions about his use of history," according to *Conversations with E.L. Doctorow*, "Doctorow intensified his claim for the artist's freedom. 'What's real and what isn't?' he rhetorically asks about the events in *Ragtime*. 'I used to know but I've forgotten.' Elsewhere he asserts that 'everything I made up about Morgan and Ford is true, whether it happened or not.'" But instead of puzzling over what is or isn't true, other critics took a widened view that centered on understanding the author's perspective on the interaction between history and fiction. They worked to analyze Doctorow's interpretation of history, how it is recorded, and how it is represented.

Many of those who lauded Doctorow's work cited widely-held beliefs dating from Aristotle's time that fiction holds a higher truth than other disciplines. Doctorow seems to support this vision, since he stated, for example, that his treatment of J. P. Morgan in *Ragtime* was "more accurate to the soul of that man than his authorized biography." Additionally, many of these critics saw literature's role as naturally subversive or opposed to history, since, in their view, history and other records are controlled by authorities with aims other than preserving human freedom. Literature can provide a logical design to history and also can provide valuable critiques, the positive critics often stated. But rather than seeing history and fiction as separate entities that converge in his work, Doctorow has made the radical comment that "there is really no fiction or nonfiction; there is only narrative."

Doctorow was also compared to authors like Twain, who questioned usual perspectives about the United States and presented a nation crippled by its corrupted ideals. In Doctorow's ragtime nation, for example, the upper class has complete control and makes quite a mess of things. In the introduction to *Conversations*, Doctorow's anti-elitist perspective is quoted: "'If I'm a leftist,' he said, 'it's because, as I think of them, the Ten Commandments is a very left dogma. What is just? What is unjust? That's where it all begins with me.'" Similarly, according to *Conversations*, Doctorow is quoted in more than one interview as calling writers "'independent witnesses' to injustice."

Curiously, while many critics celebrated the stylistic skill of the *Ragtime* narrative, it took some time before they questioned to any great degree the narrator in the book, and why Doctorow chose to not clearly identify him/her/them. It also took time for essayists to look more closely at major motifs in the work. Many had already commented on Doctorow's use of ragtime music as a symbol. The music, while first played by blacks, eventually made its way into mainstream culture. We learn that when playing the music one hand produces a repetitive piece, while the other hand plays creatively, seemingly indicative of the tension in America at the time that the novel takes place and at other times as well. Critics explored the music symbolism and examined the issue of recurrence. Similarly, they reviewed in the text the symbolism and use of film, which creates images and new methods of perceiving the world. Some saw film as symbolic of the loss of coherent representation. Many took Doctorow's use of film as well as his other stylistic devices and studied these in relation to the book's ideas about history.

Another concept later addressed by critics was Doctorow's use of transformation. Some characters in the work grow or transform (not necessarily for the better), some have the potential to do so yet do not manage it, and others are so wrapped up in their own egos that they do not even think of self-improvement. Doctorow addressed this issue in an interview in 1983. At that time he spoke not just of people's potential for improvement but of Americans' particularly unique perspective on the topic: "It seems to me we are, at least on paper, supposed to be different from, or better than, we are. And that kind of irritation confronts us all the time and has from the beginning. The Constitution was a precipitate of all the best Enlightenment thinking of Europe, and it's really quite a remarkable document. That we don't manage to live up to it is the source of all our self-analysis." The legacy of *Ragtime*, then, is to inspire humanity to be its best. Doctorow packages his message in the novel using the author's traditional methods but then goes beyond these techniques and creates an avant-garde approach to narration as well as a revolutionary technique of melding history and fiction.

List of Characters

Father is a very successful businessman, who sells fireworks, flags, and other patriotic paraphernalia. Living with his family in New Rochelle, N.Y., at times he seems a stereotypical rich white man. He is protective, helpful, and courageous, and he can be contemplative and self-aware, making him a possible example of someone who can break free of convention and/or negative traits.

Mother is Father's wife. She is the seemingly stereotypical rich white woman with a Victorian perspective, but she is also a capable businessperson, is sensitive to others, and at times is willing to take risks. She also serves as an example of someone who has the potential to break free of convention and transform.

Grandfather is Mother's father. He is a retired professor of Greek and Latin who taught Episcopal seminarians in a college in central Ohio. Now he teaches his grandson the stories of Ovid. Even as he becomes increasingly feeble, he has spunk and a love of life. He is a contrast to his daughter and her husband, as well to many other characters in the book that lack an understanding of what is truly important.

The Little Boy is the son of Mother and Father, about nine years old when the story begins. He is smart, loves saving what's been thrown away, has few friends, and is not understood by his parents. He is appealing to the reader, however, for being different and contemplative.

Mother's Younger Brother lives with the family, even though he is probably eighteen years old, if not older, when the story begins. He is a loner, in search of direction, at times depressed, and eventually a radical revolutionary. He stands as an example of someone who is willing to stand up for what is right but whose recklessness can be problematic.

Houdini is a famed escape artist, portrayed as courageous, inventive, disciplined, and having a great physique, but at the same time quite insecure and obsessed with his mother. He may be the only historical figure in the book who is truly famous but still ravenous for greater recognition. Like most of the other actual historical people in the book, he is seriously flawed, pointing to the fact that the famous, who so many respect, are really not so worthy of great respect after all.

Evelyn Nesbit is a famous beauty and artist's model. She is married to the very wealthy Harry K. Thaw and has been the mistress of Stanford White, a famous architect. She serves as an example of someone who uses her greatest asset, her beauty, to bring about her own ruin.

Harry K. Thaw, husband of Evelyn Nesbit, is part of a family that is very wealthy from coke and railroads. He is unstable, violent, and suicidal. He is living proof that money cannot solve, or even make up for, all problems.

Stanford White is a famous architect, who inadvertently causes his own death by selfishly encouraging his lover, Evelyn, to marry the very wealthy Thaw.

Tateh is a socialist Jewish immigrant from Latvia, in his early thirties when the book opens. He is married to Mameh and is determined to succeed for his daughter. For much of the book he is noble and poverty-stricken, yet later he brings about his own notable change and becomes a filmmaker, one of the few characters to transform his life.

Mameh is a Jewish immigrant, married to Tateh and mother of the Little Girl. She is extremely hard-working and has good intentions but is an example of what can happen to a person who is pushed to her limits.

The Little Girl, quiet and very beautiful, is the child of Tateh and Mameh, about eight years old when the book opens. She is a new life that grows and is still beautiful despite a near inhuman environment; she is a symbol of hope.

Jacob Riis is a journalist who exposes living conditions in the tenements and advocates rights for the poor.

Emma Goldman is a small, stout, masculine-faced famous anarchist and orator. Her function is to continually remind the downtrodden that they are powerful and to challenge other characters' views.

Sarah is a black girl who is about eighteen or nineteen years old and living with the New Rochelle family. She is willing to take another's life but is described as an innocent who is straightforward and moral. She demonstrates what can happen to a good person driven to desperation.

Coalhouse Walker Jr. is a black pianist who is well-spoken, polite, self-assured, and determined. He becomes consumed with attaining justice.

Willie Conklin is a New York fire chief, described as "a bigot so ordinary as to be like all men."

J.P. Morgan is fifty-seven years old when the novel opens, burly, and six feet tall. He is an excessively wealthy businessman with control of numerous corporations. His own inflated opinion of himself causes his discontentedness, and he becomes obsessed with reincarnation.

Henry Ford is the famed automobile manufacturer who develops the car and the assembly-line production method. While he is rich and accomplished, he speaks simply but looks down on most men. He is an example of someone who has not just inherited riches but has gained them through his own ingenuity, yet still his personality is self-serving, like most of the rich in the book.

New York District Attorney Whitman is a possible candidate for governor of New York or the U.S. presidency. He becomes a key negotiator during a major stand-off, but throughout is completely concerned about preserving his tough image. He functions as an example of how prestige, and the possibility of greater prestige, can harm a person.

Booker T. Washington is a famous black leader, who advocates that blacks advance by becoming educated and working through the system, not by agitation. His role is to offer an alternative to Walker's violence.

Summary and Analysis

Chapter 1 opens in 1902, describing a new family that moved into a house on a fashionable street in New Rochelle, New York. The family members are identified only as Father, Mother, the Little Boy, Mother's Younger Brother, and Grandfather. No family member has an individual name; instead, each one's "name" is his or her function in the family—Father, Mother, etc.—alluding to an Everyman role for each. We learn that Father earns a good living making flags, fireworks, and other patriotic items, most appropriate for the time, when, we are told, "swarms of people" attended parades, political picnics, and other such events.

The identity and status of the narrator is unclear. Many critics have decided it is the young boy in the family, although there are numerous instances where the narrator tells other characters' thoughts or knows more than we would expect a single character to know, seemingly pointing to the use of an omniscient narrator or a variety of narrators. It seems fitting that we question the narrator's identity/identities, since there is much in the book about changeability.

Background is provided on the time period of the novel; this is an era when trains, steamers, and trolleys are in use, and people wear white, carry parasols, use tennis racquets, and follow convention. "There was a lot of sexual fainting. There were no Negroes. There were no immigrants," we are told.

In this chapter the younger brother is described as a loner. He takes the trolley to the end of the line, where he can walk in the salty marshes and commune with the sea, shells, and gulls. It appears he is not so distanced from society, however, for he is in love with Evelyn Nesbit, the well-known model's artist. Her name is in all New York City newspapers, since her husband, part of a rich family, has shot and killed the famous architect Stanford White for having been Evelyn's lover. This is the first instance where the narrator interweaves actual historical persons with fictional characters and events. The technique becomes even more interesting as Doctorow adds more famous people, bringing to mind numerous questions about history and fiction.

Aside from learning about the brother in the family, we learn about the Little Boy, who is twice described here as wearing a sailor suit. The sailor suit perhaps points to the idea of sailors as living a different life from most, far away much of the time. As we learn more about the young boy, we will see how this fits his personality. This suit also shows the young boy's affinity with Mother's Younger Brother, who, as stated, likes the sea and is a loner. The boy, again like his uncle, is also enchanted with a real historical figure—Houdini, the famous escape artist. This attraction possibly points to a yearning within the boy himself, possibly for the attention Houdini gets, or possibly for the ability to escape or to do tricks. While Nesbit is now followed in the papers for the murder she brought about, Houdini is described by the narrator first in terms of his successes, and only lastly is one of his failed attempts described. "Today, nearly fifty years since his [Houdini's] death, the audience for escapes is even larger," the narrator writes, the first clear indication that this book, while written about the early 1900s, is comparing those times to "today," the mid-seventies. (Houdini died in 1926; *Ragtime* was published in 1975.)

In the very next paragraph after the quote about Houdini, Houdini's driver crashes his car into a telephone pole in front of the boy's house. We had been told that the boy had been disappointed because his family hadn't taken him to a Houdini performance, but now, instead, the performance comes to him. Father is the only one of several neighbors to offer help to Houdini and his driver. The men are invited inside the family's home, and Houdini is first described just as we wouldn't expect—modest, possibly depressed, and more impressed with Father's upcoming adventure to the Arctic with Peary than he is with his own accomplishments. At the very end of the chapter, as Houdini is ready to leave, the boy tells him, "Warn the Duke," and we have no clues what this means, nor are we told of any of the characters' reactions to it.

Chapter 2 is only two-and-a-half pages, part of the reason critics compare the book to ragtime music for its fast pace. The chapter tells of the family's preparation for the father's departure with the Peary expedition. Father has sexual desires for his wife, and they have increased, since his last experience with her had been interrupted by Houdini's accident in front of their home. This is just the first instance of the world infringing on their staid lives. When the husband and wife finally have their sexual liaison, Mother endures the experience and thinks, "Yet I know these are the happy years. And ahead of us are only great disasters." It is a great foreboding, especially since father is to embark on an arduous trip at the beginning of the novel. He will be a fictional character involved in an actual historical event, yet unless we have been schooled about the historical event we will probably find ourselves wondering if all of the details Doctorow describes are accurate. It seems here that a novelist is writing history, which raises many curious questions.

There is a great fanfare at the train station, as Father starts the first leg of his trip. Younger Brother has been told to take care of things during Father's absence and has been given a raise and more responsibility at Father's company. The next morning as Father and the others board the Peary ship, again there is a great send-off. As the ship departs, it passes a "rag ship" full of poor immigrants staring at Father. He is overtaken by a "weird despair," and the sky and ocean become dark and rough.

Chapter 3 follows the immigrants to shore, where they are treated so poorly by immigration officials and New Yorkers that they are ironically and sadly "reminded of home." Like Houdini, they were intent on escaping; Houdini is successful at his trick escapes, whereas the immigrants thought their true escapes were successful but have only entered into a new hell. They live in squalid conditions, are illiterate, and work for almost no money.

Now the reader is introduced to a new family, whose members are identified as: Mameh, Tateh, and the Little Girl in the pinafore. For this family, instead of the formal and proper "Mother" and "Father," we have a child's pronunciations of these words. Mameh and the girl work every waking moment, and the family is devastated when they find out their daughter must attend school, consequently reducing some of their already low income. In desperation, unbeknownst to the rest of the family, mother allows herself to be molested and later raped in return for some extra money from her buyer.

The famous photographer Jacob Riis is described here as he works determinedly photographing the horrid tenements; he insists that the rest of the country learn about the terrible living conditions. Mameh, Tateh, and their daughter splurge and take a ride uptown, where they see Fifth Avenue mansions Stanford White had designed. Later in the chapter, Riis goes to White to get ideas on housing for the poor. He watches as White oversees the unloading of shipments of vastly expensive architectural components, as well as fine china, rare books, and extravagant art and furniture.

Chapter 4 opens in striking contrast to the previous chapter. A politician who is running for re-election sponsors a grandly extravagant parade and party. These events end with a fireworks display, under the official supervision of Mother's Younger Brother, who has become interested in designing fireworks while working at Father's business. Brother still pines for Evelyn Nesbit, and, in fact, the rest of the chapter is devoted to her and her husband, Harry Thaw. Thaw is now in jail awaiting trial for murder. Nesbit has been practicing her testimony for her husband's defense but wonders whether a jury will find him innocent.

The lives of Nesbit, Thaw, and Stanford White are described as we hear of Thaw's violent suicidal tendencies and his beating of Nesbit prior to their marriage. White, Nesbit's lover, had recommended that she write up a statement about Thaw and bring it to a lawyer, which she promptly had done as a mechanism to get the rich Thaw to then agree to marry her. Nesbit visits her husband daily in jail, where he gets special treatment because of his wealth and continues to act despicably. Nesbit is constantly followed by reporters to whom she declares her husband's innocence. We learn that she is getting two hundred thousand dollars from Thaw for her testimony on his behalf and that she plans on getting much more from their divorce.

The site of the jail, called The Tombs, remains the focus in **chapter 5**. Houdini is summoned because the guards at The Tombs have new leg irons and challenge him to escape from them. Houdini takes advantage of the publicity opportunity, and while he is at the jail being photographed and examining the leg irons he offers his own proposal. He says he will remove his clothes and get locked in one of the most secure cells in the jail, only to escape and be back in the warden's office, completely dressed, within five minutes. The warden reluctantly agrees.

The narrator describes Houdini's escape and also discloses some of Houdini's escape secrets. While in the cell, Houdini looks across the aisle into another cell where a prisoner is staring at him. The prisoner sits in front of a white-clothed table, complete with champagne and a sumptuous meal. He has a Tiffany shade on his light, a quilt and throw pillows, and a fancy armoire. Houdini describes the man's face as that of a ventriloquist's dummy and is shocked to see him remove all of his clothes and shake his genitalia between the bars at Houdini. While Houdini had looked like an opportunist, this man tries to make fun of him but only looks like an uncouth idiot, given special treatment only because of his wealth.

Later Houdini realizes that the man in the opposite cell was Harry Thaw. Houdini is seriously upset because Thaw hadn't applauded his trick, and he thinks about his frequent failures at impressing rich people. "Always they broke through the pretense of his life and made him feel foolish," we read, seeing again an insecure Houdini, even though he had completed the impressive trick at the jail. Also, we are told, Houdini is jealous of men who fly planes and race cars; he is fascinated by modern inventions. Later, he initially turns down performing at a party for one of the richest women in New York but then relents when she increases the pay. When he arrives, he finds that she also has hired the entire side-show of the Barnum and Bailey circus. Finding himself surrounded by freaks, he leaves, refusing to be just another freak in the eyes of the very wealthy.

At the end of the chapter, Freud has just arrived in the United States and receives a weak welcome.

Chapter 6 provides more details of Freud's visit to America. He and his colleagues visit typical tourist spots such as Central Park, the Metropolitan Museum, Niagara Falls, and, more surprisingly, three amusement parks. The narrator pokes fun at Freud. For example, Freud is described as chewing on a cigar; he has trouble locating a restroom, and rides through the Tunnel of Love with Carl Jung at Luna Park. All of these occurrences seem funny in light of Freud's theories on symbols (a cigar being one of his most famous ones), his theories about people restraining from relieving themselves, and the fact that Jung was hardly a lover of Freud but broke away from him and developed his own psychological theories.

Freud leaves America in a huff. "America is a mistake, a gigantic mistake," he says. The author then explains that millions of Americans are out of work at the time, hundreds of children are mutilated each year while working with factory equipment, one hundred blacks are lynched each year, and one hundred miners are burned alive each year. This is contrasted with the lifestyles of the rich, for whom it has become "fashionable to honor the poor." Huge amounts of money are spent on gala balls where attendees dress up as the poor and the decor is a representation of a coal mine, a stockyard, or a dirt farm. Poverty has become a mechanism for entertainment.

Just as Freud had stopped on the New York streets to observe a man creating and peddling silhouettes, so too does Evelyn Nesbit in **chapter 7**. Nesbit, however, stops because the beauty of the peddler's little girl captivates her. Around the girl's waist is a rope that is tied to her father to prevent her from being stolen, a common problem in the Jewish slums at the time, according to another man on the street. We also learn that Nesbit thinks the peddler, revealed as Tateh, is old because of his gray hair, but he is only thirty-two and has disowned his wife for selling her body.

Nesbit is so taken with the young girl that she stops in the street each day, wearing an old shawl over her head to hide her identity. Tateh create silhouettes for her, and he makes so many that he becomes proficient in also adding creative details in the background. "Most of these are today in private collections," the narrator tells us, again, one of the few times he makes us aware that we are not just to be thinking about the early 1900s. Also, by mentioning that these silhouettes created by a fictional character are in private collections, we are forced again to think about the differentiation between fiction and history.

Nesbit visits the child every afternoon, always dressing in shabby clothes. The reporters who had so closely followed Nesbit have yet to determine where she's been going, so they invent new scandalous stories about her. Ironically, these stories are told just at the point when she is showing some genuine compassion, but that compassion is unknown to the public. Nesbit, who is described as being "desperately in love" with the young girl, notices that she has a secret admirer who has been following her—Mother's Younger Brother. Nesbit learns where Tateh and his child live, and she goes there when she doesn't find them on the street one day. She takes care of the child who has become sick, so Tateh can work. Nesbit considers kidnapping the child (the very thing the people on the streets had told her was a major problem in these slums) and leaving Tateh on his own.

In **chapter 8**, Tateh, president of the Socialist Artists' Alliance, takes Nesbit to a meeting that this group sponsors to raise money for strikers in other locations. Emma Goldman, the stout and feisty famed anarchist, is the speaker. She preaches against marriage, saying it weakens women and is akin to prostitution, which causes an uproar of disagreement from the crowd. She continues to explain how women suffer from a lack of freedom and respect, and when her eyes alight on Nesbit in the audience, whose shawl has fallen from her head, Goldman tells the group that among them is a prime example of her point. Goldman says this woman is one of the most brilliant in America, that she worked the capitalist system with her sexual beauty and yet is viewed as scandalous. Goldman doesn't identify Nesbit to the audience; many strain to determine who Goldman is referring to, but Tateh does make the connection. Just as the police enter and pandemonium ensues, he casts an ugly contemptuous gaze at Nesbit, calling her a whore and fleeing with his daughter.

Goldman grabs Nesbit, and they escape by a back stairway and are followed by Mother's Younger Brother back to Goldman's place in a rooming house. He manages to slip into a closet in the room without the women knowing. Goldman explains that she has admired Nesbit for a long time but couldn't always understand why. Goldman says, "Who can say who are the instrumentalities and who are the people. Which of us causes, and lives in others to cause, and which of us is meant thereby to live. That is exactly my point." Goldman tells her that she once tried to be a prostitute to obtain money needed for a revolutionary cause, but she ended up just being given money by an old man who told her to stop the prostitution, which she did. Goldman's words about people and instruments seem to be the thoughts of Doctorow himself, who created a work where amazing coincidences occur and thereby point out the interconnectedness of people and events. At the same time, the words seem to address Doctorow's technique of melding fictional characters and real people in the work. In this book, the real people often have minor parts when compared to the fictional characters; the "real," then, may be just the instruments in his story.

When Goldman realizes Nesbit is wearing a confining corset, she undresses her. Goldman rubs her with alcohol and massages her body that is reddened from the metal stays. Nesbit becomes sexually aroused, and Mother's Younger Brother, whom we have almost forgotten is in the closet, falls out of the closet feverish with desire.

Chapter 9 returns to Mother—head of the household and forced to run the family's business since her husband is still away—worrying because her brother has disappeared. She has spoken to him since he has been in New York City, but he basically gives her no information; she doesn't know when he will come back home and she becomes furious. Mother wishes she could confide her worries in her father, but he is now ninety and removed from life. She thinks back to the years when he was a professor of Greek and Latin and thinks about their less encumbered surroundings; she remembers taking care of her brother even then, and of playing in the hayloft. Now she feels "deserted by the race of males and furious with herself for the nostalgia that [sweeps] through her" frequently while her husband is away.

Fleeing to the garden for solace, Mother instead literally stumbles upon another problem. She begins digging when she hears something in the ground. The maid screams and the boy sees Mother's face turn horribly old and ugly. Only then does he see that she has dug up a small newborn black baby. The women are hysterical. Mother calls the doctor and the police, and very shortly the police find the mother of the baby, a poor washwoman. Mother sees the washwoman's beautiful face and is shocked by how young she is. As the woman and child are about to be taken away and Mother hears their probable fate, she says she will take care of them instead. She is disturbed and again frustrated that her husband is not there to help and that she cannot communicate with him. She feels that the girl and her child have brought to the family "a sense of misfortune," "chaos," and "contamination." The sun sets "blood red."

While Mother feels desperate for communication with her husband, in **chapter 10** he is contentedly writing daily in his journal and living in "surprising comfort." Peary, bigoted and selfish, lives in extravagance, having brought a player piano along in his stateroom. While he compares the Eskimos to dogs, he uses their survival techniques, calling them his own survival system and bragging about it. Father, too, sees the Eskimos as primitives and is especially shocked to see a woman actively participating in sex. He mentally compares her to his fastidious, intelligent, well-groomed wife. The sun, when it finally appears, is "misshapen" and blood red, just as it had been after the unsettling events that were described in the previous chapter.

The trip becomes grueling and the weather unbearable, even, at times, for the Eskimos accompanying the group. The narrator describes the arduous trip as the men get closer and closer to their goal, and only later do we learn that Father "had long since gone back" because parts of his extremities kept freezing, the "fate of some men" traveling in the North. Peary had told Father he must go home, even though Father's society had donated much money to the trip and even though the two men got along quite well, and especially after having found out that they both had belonged to the same fraternity years ago. Peary is relentless in driving the remaining men to the Pole, and ironically, once near the location he cannot detect where the actual North Pole is. Adding to the irony is the fact that the photo of the men who make it shows only dark circles for faces, with no specific person being distinguishable.

In **chapter 11**, Nesbit has taken Mother's Younger Brother as her lover, and the relationship is almost purely sexual. They hardly talk, bringing to mind the two previous chapters showing the lack of communication between Mother and Father. We also are reminded of the poor communication between Mother and her brother when she spoke with him on the phone from New York. Men do not need conversation, and women, even Nesbit, as we will find by the end of the chapter, are desperate for communication, especially with men. Ironically, for Nesbit, the only man she had been able to really communicate with was White, the man whose murder she had caused.

Thaw's trial has begun and Nesbit performs beautifully during her testimony, as she had promised she would for payment. Her stunning image appears on every newspaper, selling out the papers when it appears on the front page. "Her testimony created the first sex goddess in American history," we are told, and movie men realize that more people will attend their films if they feature women like Nesbit.

When the jury on the Thaw case cannot make a decision, another trial is held, and Nesbit performs her practiced testimony once again. This time Thaw is ordered to an asylum for the criminally insane. Nesbit sues for her one-million-dollar divorce, only to end up with twenty-five thousand instead, as a result of her affair with Mother's Younger Brother and other men who Thaw's lawyers "made up." Goldman warns Nesbit that she will waste the small portion of money she's received, and Nesbit believes it. She gives money away anonymously to radical causes. She is terribly unhappy, wishing she were with a man "who would treat her badly and whom she could treat badly."

"And what of Tateh and his little girl?"—so begins **chapter 12**. This is the type of sentence that begins some chapters and what some critics see as a weak transition and an indication of Doctorow's lack of skill in connecting his disparate stories and characters. Looking beyond such criticism, though, we see that such a sentence speaks directly to the readers, reminding us that a person is telling a story according to his or her own style and timeframe. So the story continues, in yet another relatively short chapter, as if a short scene in a play, or, as some have said, as if a short imagistic section of a film.

Tateh has decided he must leave New York, the city that he believes has ruined him. He distributes the only money he has—thirty dollars—among his pockets and shoes and boards the streetcar with his daughter, with no idea of where they will go. The wind is cold against them, and in the middle of the paragraph there is an interruption in the story: "There was in these days of our history a highly developed system of interurban street railway lines. One could travel great distances on hard rush seats or wooden benches by taking each line to its terminus and transferring to the next." The next two sentences interrupt to narrate some of "our history," reinforcing the idea that this book is not just a novel but also a historical text. But, beyond this, the author writes not just history, but a part of "our" history, making us an outgrowth of the tale and making the entire story more immediate.

Tateh and his daughter reach the end of the line and get on the next streetcar. The sun shines, and the conductors smile. The two travelers continue all the way to New Rochelle. The pair plans to travel through, but still they must get off and transfer, and while waiting for the transfer "a boy and his mother" pass by. The little girl looks at the boy, who has a sailor suit on, and so we assume he is the Little Boy, just as we anticipated. But the reader is teased here, for the girl continues to watch the boy until he is out of site, but no further connection occurs. Tateh and his daughter continue riding into

Connecticut. They pass open fields and grazing cows, and Tateh realizes his daughter is happy. Tateh smiles for the first time in a long time, and he decides they will at least go as far as Boston.

Chapter 13 starts with an exclamation about the number of rail tracks now covering the country and explains that yet another engineering feat was taking place. To accommodate more underground trains, a tunnel is being built from Brooklyn to the Battery. At this site a horrible accident occurs, an explosion so powerful it forces four workmen out of the tunnel, through twenty feet of silt, and through the river out onto a geyser. Only one of the men survives, and Houdini tracks him down in his hospital bed to hear his account of the accident.

"The real world act was what got into history books," Houdini thinks, as he ponders the accident. Note the use of the word "act," drawing to mind the connotation of something staged. Also, Doctorow again forces us to rethink history; after all, only some things make it into the history books, depending on the author of the book and the historical event. Houdini decides to focus on performing outdoor tricks and also decides to return to Europe to perform. He, like the immigrant Tateh, still feels more at home and more accepted in his native land. He continues to perform tricks before leaving but is dissatisfied. He is very upset about leaving his mother but receives some consolation from being appreciated by European audiences and newspapers. Still, though, he remains discontented.

One day Houdini sees a demonstration of a French-made flying machine and buys one for himself, along with the services of a mechanic who also provides him with flying lessons. While flying, Houdini finally feels free and grand. The plane's engine is described as "better than the one the Wrights themselves were using," a jab at modern America. Houdini is asked to show his flying skill for a man in a brilliant white car with a flag on its fender. Not knowing who the man is, but knowing he must be important, Houdini shows his skill and afterwards is allowed by the car, where he meets its rider,

Archduke Franz Ferdinand, heir to the Austro-Hungarian throne. The archduke sits with "stupid heavy-lidded eyes" and mistakenly congratulates Houdini not on his flying but on his invention of the plane. This ends part one of the three sections that the book is divided into.

Chapter 14 describes Father's return to a very different home, "finding everywhere signs of his own exclusion." There are two new people in the house, as well as new items, and almost everyone in it has grown. Father, however, is weaker, and treated as a convalescent. Gaunt and round-shouldered, he limps, and his body seems impossible to warm. He pulls numerous presents for the family from his bags, yet the gifts seem inappropriate, as if "possessions of a savage." Indeed Father feels like a savage himself, feeling guilty about having had sex with an Eskimo woman. He is surprised to find his wife now much more sexually open and discovers material about women's liberation and limiting family size next to their bed.

Additionally, Father is "astounded" when he learns how his wife has expertly handled the business in his absence. Also, Father is surprised to learn that her brother spends many hours a day working, designing new fireworks. Brother brings Father to the salt marshes to demonstrate his new "cherry bomb" explosive, and Father is alarmed when he sees its power. We learn also that the brother's relationship with Nesbit is over. She had left him a note saying she was going off with a professional ragtime dancer, and he mourns her loss. He has a crate of silhouette portraits left from their relationship and a pair of Evelyn's shoes she had discarded. One day in anger he throws the crate and shoes away, but they are retrieved by his nephew.

In **chapter 15**, we learn that the Little Boy "treasured anything discarded." He picks one silhouette of Tateh's daughter and hangs it on the inside of his wardrobe door. While a smart child, the boy is described as learning nothing in school and having no friends, prompting his mother to believe him strange and wish him "ordinary." While in the previous chapter she has demonstrated growth, here we see that in certain respects she is still conventional.

Grandfather, while quite deteriorated, spends time telling the boy stories from Ovid about transformations—women and men change into sunflowers, or animals, or just thin air. At times, as Grandfather speaks, he drifts from English to Latin, as if before one of his college classes from forty years ago; this again brings to mind the idea of transformation or changeability and one's lack of control over it. "... [I]t appeared nothing was immune to the principle of volatility, not even language," Doctorow writes. This and a few of his other key ideas are touched on in this chapter, more compactly and directly than in other parts of the book.

Aside from change and volatility, repetition is discussed in the context of technology, another key force throughout the book. The boy enjoys both moving picture shows and playing records over and over; for him repetition is comforting. Also curious here is the comment that films "depended on the capacity of humans, animals or objects to forfeit portions of themselves." Change, then, requires loss, just as it did in the stories of Ovid.

The boy takes to looking in the mirror, "expecting some change to take place before his eyes." This is a curious contrast to the actions of Father, who, upon returning from his trip with Peary is shocked to see himself look different in the mirror at home than in the one he had on his trip, and who is also shocked by his transformation to a severely physically deteriorated state. The father, then, appears less wise than his son, not only for being unaware of his own change on the trip but for not anticipating it in light of the formidable journey toward the Pole. While the boy is open to fictional allegories of change, the father does not accept change or growth well. He has gone on the trip, yet the family has grown, not him.

The boy also looks to the mirror "as a means of self-duplication" and receives from it a "sensation of being disembodied," again reinforcing earlier comments in the chapter. Similarly, the boy speaks of attending the unveiling of a new statue, again a symbol of replication and transformation. He points out that even a solid statue does not stay the same but is subjected to weathering. "It was evident to him," we are told, "that the world composed and recomposed itself constantly in an endless process of dissatisfaction." Again change has negative associations, although it is curious that the word "dissatisfaction" is used, indicating not necessarily that the change has been bad but that it produces a dissatisfied reaction.

The final description in the chapter is of Mother, Younger Brother, and the Little Boy ice skating, an outing that the mother believes will be good for them since it takes place outside, is pleasant, and not solitary. The scene is described as "merry," yet it becomes slightly sour as the focus turns first to the "constant cut-cut" of the skates and second to the boy's vision of the skate tracks as being constantly erased, dissolving the past and its journeys.

In **chapter 16**, we find Tateh and his daughter in a mill town in Massachusetts, living nearly as sorry an existence as they had in New York City. When the owners of one of the mills hand out smaller pay than usual, the workers there and in the rest of the town strike. Tateh, who had been working in one of the mills for the standard measly salary, joins in the strikes, which wear on for weeks. At night Tateh draws for his daughter to entertain her and devises a booklet of a series of images that look like they are moving when the booklet's pages are thumbed. He wonders if he will ever be able to do much more for her.

The strikes become famous, and organizers devise a plan to allow the workers' children to be taken temporarily into the homes of volunteers in nearby cities. When the first hundred children arrive at the train station to be transported to new temporary quarters, they receive enormous press coverage and the mill owners realize they can never again allow another scene showing the poor children. Tateh vacillates but then decides it would be best if his daughter leaves with the next group of children. When the appointed day comes, Tateh arrives at the station, where there are numerous other parents and children—as well as militia with rifles. Chaos breaks out as the militia and additional police separate the parents from their children. People are trampled, beaten, and bleeding. Tateh lifts his daughter onto the back of the train and goes back into the turmoil to help a fallen woman, only to be beaten himself until he too falls. When the police and militia clear out, Tateh hears his child's voice calling him. She is on the last car of the train, just beyond the station, and when Tateh sees that the train is starting to move he runs after it, managing to catch the guardrail of the observation platform.

Once pulled inside the train by two conductors in **chapter 17**, Tateh sees that he is injured and bleeding. A doctor takes care of him and gives him an injection that nearly knocks him out for the trip to Philadelphia. Upon arriving there, Tateh reads a discarded newspaper and sees that the turmoil at the Massachusetts train station has brought in the federal government and victory for the strikers. Yet, he assumes wages will be raised only ever so slightly and will still make his and his daughter's lives unbearable. He decides there is no point in their returning to the mill town and begins to envision a life better than what they had and separate from the working class. "I hate machines," he says, a rather un-American comment in light of the fact that America was in the midst of a technological revolution that most equated with rapid advancement and improved quality of life. As Tateh and his daughter walk through Philadelphia, they see extravagant shops but also a novelty shop. Tateh walks in, shows the man there his booklet of pictures that look like they're moving when you flip the pages, sells it for twenty-five dollars, and gets a contract for four more. The company calls the invention "movie books."

In **chapter 18** we are told that workers might strike and die but entrepreneurs will always manage. Examples of entrepreneurship at the lowest end of the economic scale are given, and then the setting moves to a factory, but as it is seen through the eyes of its owner rather than its workers. The owner watches a Model T roll off an assembly line. We are told that he is the car's inventor—another real historical figure, Henry Ford. Ford chews on a piece of straw as he checks over the car, appearing rather down-to-earth, but then he takes from his pocket a gold watch, and we read that "he had long believed that most human beings were too dumb to make a living." He is not just rich and inventive, but, like many of the other wealthy real figures in the book, he is prejudiced. He is ecstatic here, not from having invented the car but from having invented the assembly line. "He had caused a machine to replicate itself endlessly," Doctorow writes. The issue of duplication is a key theme throughout the book. For America at the time there seems a safety in sameness. But we are told that not only are the parts of the cars interchangeable from one car to the next, but the people working on the assembly line are interchangeable as well. Men are dehumanized and become like machines.

In **chapter 19**, we are informed that Ford is not "at the top of the business pyramid. Only one man occupied that lofty place." That man is J. P. Morgan, the fifty-seven-year-old who was born into wealth and then amassed an even greater fortune. In the beginning of the chapter, Morgan wants to meet Henry Ford. Morgan has met many people yet believes no one is as preeminent as he. It is disturbing to him that he is so far above others, that Rockefeller and Carnegie and other powerful men in the world, for example, fall asleep over their drinks or speak of their constipation. He believes they have nothing of value to say. One wonders how they have, in fact, made it to their elite posts. Doctorow describes their wives, saying "the hard pull of rampant achievement had sucked the life out of their flesh." For these, then, there has been a price to pay for their prestige; they have lost themselves. Morgan embarks on intense studies of the past, believing that he may find some answers there. He becomes intrigued when a guide at the Great Pyramid tells him that into each age sacred heroes are born to help the rest of man. Morgan decides that he and Ford are in this category of heroes.

In **chapter 20**, Ford has lunch with Morgan and is then escorted into Morgan's extravagant library that houses his collections of rare treasures. Morgan takes Ford through a hidden passageway to a room no one but Morgan has ever entered. The room holds the ultimate treasures gained as a result of his obsession about the Egyptian wisdom he learned at the pyramid. One of the treasures is a sarcophagus and an effigy of an ancient king with a striking resemblance to Ford himself. Morgan explains his research into the godlike heroes and secret wisdom.

Morgan comments on the dangers of machinery when he says, "… [O]nly in the age of science have these men and their wisdom dropped from view. I'll tell you why: The rise of mechanistic science, of Newton and Descartes, was a great conspiracy, a great devilish conspiracy to destroy our apprehension of reality and our awareness of the transcendentally gifted among us." It is curious that while he had praised Ford earlier, the man who devised the assembly-line auto, here he reveals his own prejudice against a mechanized society. We are reminded of Tateh's statement against machines; now we hear the same sentiment from a learned man at the top of the economic strata. Morgan finally ends his speech with a request that Ford go with him to Egypt. Ford explains in his very matter-of-fact and unrefined manner that he learned all he needed to know about reincarnation years ago from a book he bought for only twenty-five cents. He will not go on the trip but does concede "the possibility of an awesome lineage."

Anything Egyptian is now fashionable in **chapter 21**. Mother changes the décor in the dining room to an Egyptian pattern, and her son becomes entranced with magazines about thieved tombs and mummies' curses. The chapter then focuses on a new character who drives up the family's street, Broadview Avenue, in a shiny car. The situation is reminiscent of Houdini's arrival, although this driver is not famous, at least not yet. He is Coalhouse Walker Jr. and is looking for Sarah, the black girl the family has taken in. But when Sarah hears of his arrival, she asks that the family send him away. Mother sees in Walker "something disturbingly resolute and self-important" when she first greets him. Then she is quite angry when after speaking with Sarah and returning to the kitchen she finds the black man cooing over the baby in the carriage, rather than standing outside behind the closed door where she had left him.

Walker appears the following Sunday as well, and continues

to come each week, never showing frustration when he hears that Sarah again will not see him. Mother sees the visits as hopeful, while Father sees them as a nuisance. Mother decides to invite Walker into the parlor for tea, and again Father is disturbed, especially when he sees that the man is not uncomfortable, deferential, or in awe. Walker is a pianist, Mother and Father find out, and they invite him to play. He sits down to the family's piano and tells them it is out of tune; Father is embarrassed, but Mother admits they are never good at keeping up with it. By the time the first song is done, all the rest of the family, but not Sarah, have come to see who is the great pianist playing the ragtime piece. There are more weeks of visits and no response from Sarah, but then she gives in and then finally accepts Walker's proposal of marriage. Doctorow writes: "The appearance of these magnificent lovers in the family's life had been startling; the conflict of their wills had exercised an almost hypnotic effect." The family is being pulled out of its usual, safe world.

Chapter 22 switches back to troubled love. Mother's Younger Brother has started visiting New York City. He finds Emma Goldman's residence and goes with her to a meeting in support of the Mexican Revolution. "He hadn't known there was a Mexican Revolution," we are told, showing us that even Brother, who is the most rebellious in the family, has a limited perspective. The revolutionaries need guns, and this rebellious loner with access to explosives seems a perfect candidate to aid in a revolution.

Yet Mother's Younger Brother is focused on Goldman. She tells the listeners that the Mexicans are not foreigners. "There is only one struggle throughout the world, there is only the flame of freedom trying to light the hideous darkness of life on earth," she shouts, voicing Doctorow's perspective in favor of the downtrodden. She receives great applause.

Brother follows Goldman at the reception after her speech, yet he only gets her attention after everyone is gone. Just as she offered sage counsel to Evelyn Nesbit, she does the same for him, telling him he must take care of himself and stop pining over Nesbit, since they never would have been happy anyway.

He says she offers good advice but cries as he listens to her, and afterwards on the train home he imagines throwing himself under its wheels.

Whereas in chapter 22 widespread violence is described that is far away, in **chapter 23** trouble starts right in New York and involves a familiar character. Coalhouse Walker is stopped in front of the Emerald Isle volunteer fire house, where some of the firemen block his way and tell him he must pay a toll. Fire Chief Conklin makes a derogatory remark to Walker, who then asks two black boys to watch his car while he gets the police.

The policeman offers no help, and when Walker goes back to the fire station his car is in the field next to the road, mud spattered, with a ripped roof and human excrement on the back seat. Walker tells the firemen he wants the car cleaned and repaired, and they laugh at him. Two police arrive, and Walker is arrested. He calls the family to bail him out, goes to work, and the next morning tells them all the details of the incident, calmly and objectively.

Sarah listens to the story out of sight of the rest of the group, appearing invisible even though she is now an integral part of Walker's life. Strong forebodings come in the form of her thoughts: "She perceived as no one in the family could the enormity of the misfortune." Father gruffly says he will pay for Walker's lawyer, "if he intended to pursue his claim," still not realizing that a man like Walker doesn't give up. The car now has broken lights and glass, flat rear tires, destroyed cushions, and a roof "slashed to ribbons."

In **chapter 24** Mother's Younger Brother is trying to keep from sinking in total unhappiness or from having a nervous collapse. His sister and her husband view his actions as just new eccentricities. When he is at home in the evening, they invite him into the parlor with them, but he states, "He felt he couldn't breathe." These are nearly the same words that Tateh uses a number of chapters earlier when he feels there is no hope for him in New York City.

The chapter switches to background on Walker, which the narrator says the reader should learn, "given subsequent events" and even though little information is available. He was born in St. Louis to parents that are unknown, and he saved to pay for his own piano lessons. It is possible that he was divorced. No records exist regarding his education or indicating how he learned to speak so well. The narrator writes: "It was widely reported when he was achieving his notoriety that Coalhouse Walker had never exhausted the peaceful and legal means of redress before taking the law into his own hands." We realize that Walker's notoriety will arise from violence. Again, the narrator returns to speaking of the action of the book as if it is actual historical event, telling us what is "reported," as if by unbiased observers of events.

Walker consults three lawyers, who all tell him "to forget the matter." Father also makes an unsuccessful attempt to call a lawyer on his behalf. Walker is laughed at when he attempts to file the necessary papers against the firemen on his own. The narrator warns of events to come when he states, "Later, when the name Coalhouse Walker came to symbolize murder and arson...." This inspires the reader to read faster. Indeed, some critics have chastised Doctorow for creating a novel with a fast pace; yet others remind us that the book's epigraph is a quote from Scott Joplin, warning musicians to never play ragtime fast. Hence it seems that Doctorow is warning us not to read his ragtime book too fast as well. Even though we may be hungry for the plot, we will miss too much if we read too quickly.

Near the end of the chapter, Father tells Walker that he should have backed down about the car long ago. Hearing this, Younger Brother cannot contain himself and rebukes Father: "You speak like a man who has never been tested in his principles." This is the first time the brother has spoken out against the family, indicating his growth and desire to no longer be constrained.

Chapter 25 focuses on Sarah. Believing she can help Walker, she sneaks off to a gathering where a candidate on the national Republican ticket will be giving a speech. She assumes she can obtain some help from this powerful man and waits, shoeless, as numerous dignitaries arrive in front of the hotel where the speech will take place. Many militiamen are there, especially leery since President McKinley and New York City's mayor have been assassinated and since someone attempted to kill Theodore Roosevelt. When Sarah sees the candidate, she reaches her hand out to him, calling him, and a member of the militia butts her as hard as he can with his weapon. She falls over, and a Secret Service man jumps on her. She is brought to jail and only the next morning, when the police sergeant is concerned that she has been coughing up blood, is she taken to a doctor. Sarah is hospitalized, and by week's end she is dead.

Chapter 26 describes Sarah's lavish funeral. Most in attendance are well-dressed musicians and their female partners. Riding with the mourners on the way to the cemetery is a tuxedoed five-piece brass band in an open omnibus. They ride slowly from Harlem through to Brooklyn. People on the sidewalks stare; passengers on passing trolleys stand up as the procession goes by. It may be the first time in the book that a minority receives notable, non-negative attention.

The exclamation "Spring!, spring!" begins **chapter 27**. It is a striking departure from the end of the previous chapter and apparently is urging us to believe in growth and hope. Grandfather is so joyful because of the spring growth and beauty that he attempts a dance, falls, fractures his pelvis, "and entered a period of declining health from which he would not recover." Hope is fleeting, then, in Doctorow's world, although we are told that Grandfather keeps smiling even while in pain.

We are also informed in this chapter that another character has been suffering. Houdini, has been distraught ever since his mother's death some months earlier. He is distressed over the fact that she called his name repeatedly only moments before she died, and he believes she must have had something highly important to tell him. He knows spiritual fraud is everywhere but sets on a quest to find a way to contact his mother. Recharged by this goal, he again takes up performing, but now his shows are so extreme that audiences are frequently horrified. "Every feat enacted Houdini's desire for his dead mother," we read. "He was buried and reborn, buried and reborn." Death and rebirth images occur throughout the book, yet here the image is massively distorted and rebirth is not positive. This outlook ties in as well with Doctorow's frequent tales within the book regarding technology; man is so enchanted by technology, but it does not always bring improvement. The chapter ends with the conclusion of one of Houdini's distressing tricks. There is a huge explosion.

At the beginning of **chapter 28**, we learn that the explosion actually comes from the Emerald Isle firehouse. Detectives have pieced together the details leading up to the explosion, but they do not know who caused the disaster. Apparently the firemen were just leaving the firehouse, responding to an alarm. Upon exiting the station, the horses pulling the men and their equipment were fatally shot, as were all but one of the men. This man was crushed and killed by the steam boiler that had fallen when the horses panicked. The flaming coals from the engine's firebox then destroyed the firehouse in a blaze, ironically. This in turn caused the boiler to explode and to send burning wood soaring into the nearby field. The next evening, the newspaper reports that the perpetrator is believed to be a "Negro" man and that he is looking for Fire Chief Conklin.

The scene moves to discussions in the family's house, where Father lashes out at his wife for having "victimized" them all by taking in the baby and Sarah in the first place. He says he will go to the police in the morning. Mother's Younger Brother challenges him, saying he must tell the police the whole story behind the destruction of Walker's car, how no one was concerned with his justice, and how Sarah died. "Would you defend this savage?" Father asks his brother-in-law incredulously. And Brother fights back, pale and trembling, while the baby cries.

The family does not know that Walker has actually already identified himself, leaving letters at two newspaper offices. The letters delineate his demands that his car be returned in its proper condition and that Conklin be handed over to him. Otherwise, the letter states, other firemen and firehouses will be destroyed, as well as the whole city, if necessary. In the morning, Father, described here as widely respected in the community, goes to the police. There has been great destruction, and the family, too, is crumbling. Beyond this, there is the warning of possibly more destruction to come, and in light of many other events in the book, we expect the additional destruction to come and to have severe consequences. This ends part two of the book.

Chapter 29 opens with a description of Father's childhood. While born into a family with money, his mother died young and his father gambled their fortune away and died. As a result, Father left Harvard. He was "cautious, sober, industrious and chronically unhappy." Yet he was smart and became a successful businessman. The description makes us sympathize with Father and respect him, which is a different view from the previous chapter. Father is accustomed to taking action and succeeding, but he struggles now as life moves beyond his control.

The reader's perspective of Father develops further: "He wondered if his dislike for Coalhouse Walker, which had been instantaneous, was based not on the man's color but on his being engaged in an act of courtship, a suspenseful enterprise that suggested the best of life was yet to come." Father, then, is not so closed-minded as we originally suspected. He has lashed out against his family members; and yet, now this patriarch is willing to analyze his faults. In the process he discovers his own jealousy for a black man that he normally would have viewed as beneath him. Father thinks, also, about his own aging and about his deteriorating relationship with his wife. But he doesn't just think, he acts. For when he goes to the police he does take his brother-in-law's advice and explains that Walker is a peaceful man driven mad by unjust circumstances.

The police, desperate for information, ask Father to spend as much time there as he can. Chief Conklin also appears in the station, and Father is disgusted by his demeanor and advice that they "wipe out once and for all" all "niggers." Yet while Father is repulsed, the police are uninterested and teasing, consistent with earlier police reactions. Conklin goes so far as to gather armed men to surround his home, even though police are already stationed there, an action that only adds more volatility to the situation. The station, too, is described as disgusting, filled with vile language and criminals, seemingly far removed from law and order.

Father notices that Conklin, even with the security at his house, is spending much time at the station, probably out of fear. Father himself is there quite often, thereby showing him to be not so completely different from the disgusting Conklin after all. Father, however, appears oblivious to the comparison, seemingly back to his old self rather than the more open, contemplative self revealed earlier in the chapter.

Within a week after the firehouse tragedy, a second attack occurs at another firehouse. Again more men are killed and the firehouse is destroyed. City inhabitants are now panicked and outraged, not just at Conklin but at the city's administrators. Militia arrive from New York City. As information spreads, the family's home becomes surrounded, first with reporters and then with "sightseers." While the house is described as "stifling," only Mother is seen as falling apart, regressing to her stereotyped weak female role. She bitterly questions why Father can't hire more household help for her, alluding to his cheapness, which she had never done before.

The chapter ends with Father thinking again, possibly the most extensive self-examiner in the book. The chapter itself is longer than most of the others, slowing down the book's fast pace. "Coalhouse ruled," we are told, while Father feels completely helpless. He finds flaws in his relationships with each member of his family due to his own mistakes and begins to see hints of his own father within him. He "condemned himself most" for neglecting his son and acts on it, inviting him to a baseball game he knows the boy is interested in.

Chapter 30 relates the events at the baseball game, narrated mostly from the father's perspective. The father and son take public transportation and become excited by the energy by the ballpark; it is a great relief to be out of their surrounded house. The game is close, and the crowd is passionate. The teams fight repeatedly and the fans also join in by throwing bottles onto the field.

Father recalls the gentlemanly Harvard ball games of his past and is disturbed to find himself nostalgic when he had always viewed himself as progressive. "He thought, for instance," we read, that "there was no reason the Negro could not with proper guidance carry every burden of human achievement.... He felt his father's loss of fortune had the advantage of saving him from the uncritical adoption of the prejudices of his class." The hope that Father could be progressive seems to be waning here.

Father asks his son what he likes about the game, and the son replies that it is the repetition of the pitcher throwing the ball so as to fool the batter. Numerous critics point this out as another example of the boy, who many believe is the narrator in his early life, voicing Doctorow's fascination with repetition. History repeating itself is a common belief, and Doctorow's book implies that the 1970s (when the book is published) are a repetition of the early 1900s; humanity is repeating its own mistakes, not only individually but as a society. Alternatively, repetition can provide a base of steadiness for the experimental. In ragtime music, as the left hand repeats, the right hand can be innovative; so too some repetition in the world provides stability as the world struggles to grow.

Another aspect of the boy's comment has to do with fooling. When the boy's father says that sometimes the batter hits the ball, the boy responds that in these instances the batter has fooled the pitcher. Either someone is the fooler or someone is being fooled, but there is a fluidity to the situation. One party, then, is not always in charge, an idea that provides some hope, perhaps, for the downtrodden. The boy's statement does occur after Walker has managed to take power away from city authorities. And throughout the book, while the disadvantaged may not always gain, the powerful are usually shown as seriously flawed and potentially unstable.

In **chapter 31**, the baseball game is over and Father panics, thinking he shouldn't have left his wife home alone. Yet the emotion is erased when he bonds with his son on the trolley ride home—the boy takes his hand and Father puts his arm around his shoulders, repeating Tateh's own experience with his daughter. When Father and son arrive home, Mother is in great spirits as well. She shows them that Sarah's baby is now walking everywhere triumphantly.

Mother and Father become close again. Both of them have been pulled out of their ill humor by something external, a naturally occurring life joy. They speak frankly that night about the family's current circumstances, the need to get away, and the issues that make that difficult. Father tells his wife to let him take care of everything, and she is grateful. They make love, and she is so loving and encouraging that he, for the first time in months, feels she appreciates him. The tension is relieved in the house to a great degree, albeit by the traditional method of the husband taking control and his wife serving as a support.

The family prepares to leave for Atlantic City. In the meantime, the situation in the city around them intensifies. Newsmen press for Walker's car to be removed from the pond, and when photos of the ruined and waterlogged vehicle appear in the papers, people throng to see it and are appalled. Embarrassed, the mayor and aldermen issue further condemnations against the "colored madman." But the city's inhabitants focus on Conklin, calling for him to leave, with some threatening to take action against him themselves.

Conklin remains out of touch with the people, and believes that he should be amassing "the most profound admiration" for his actions. "He felt martyred by what he called the nigger lovers, even though these now seemed to constitute virtually the entire population of the city." Helpless, he drinks himself into a stupor, while his wife and others prepare to leave. It is one of the few semblances of justice to occur. The newspapers and the people have produced positive action, while the authorities remain more concerned with their own reputations.

The chapter ends with a focus again on the family, who somehow have managed to leave without anyone taking notice. They have new baggage, Mother wears "a white ensemble," and there is optimism as they wait in the vast and impressive New York Pennsylvania Station, even though it was built, we are told, by Stanford White's firm, which reminds us of White's ugly story.

The story returns to Mother's Younger Brother in **chapter 32**. After his confrontation with Father he disappeared from the house and never returned, even though he has at times gone to work. But the family is not concerned, since they see these recent actions as appropriate to brother's "sullen temper." Several days after the first firehouse attack Younger Brother started to track down Walker. When he eventually gets access to Walker in a brownstone basement, he tells Walker he can make bombs for him. Brother takes materials from Father's factory, shaves his head and moustache, blackens his face (appealing to Walker's followers' sense of irony), and is accepted when his first bomb works at the second firehouse attack.

The narrator informs us that information about brother is derived from a diary he kept from the day he joined Walker's revolutionary group to the day he died in Mexico about a year later. This raises questions about the need for the narrator to provide source material to support a fictional character's story.

Walker has a small group of highly devoted followers who dress just like him and even call each other by his name. They pool their money, share responsibilities, and discuss future plans. As part of this group, Brother "awoke every day into a state of solemn joy," transformed from his previous life. Walker, too, physically transforms, shaving his head and moustache after his photo appeared in the newspapers. Brother sees this as "a ritualistic grooming for the final battle." The orderly scene describing Walker's followers contrasts with the confusion and panic of the city at large. From any perspective, though, the situation appears to be reaching a climax.

We expect **chapter 33** to be related to the turmoil of the city; instead, it discusses the beauty of the family's summer at the beach. So much is light, white, and fresh here, a markedly different world from Walker's basement in the brownstone. At the hotel there are white starched tablecloths and multiple-course meals. Here the family "felt they looked grand and prosperous." It isn't even enough, then, for them to be grand and prosperous, the pleasure comes in feeling that others see them that way.

Mother is excessively modest when wearing her bathing attire and only gets slightly wet in the surf, while her husband's suit is immodest and he takes great pleasure in swimming far out. After swimming the couple makes love if Mother allows it, but it is different from the last sexual episode described, because Mother has lost faith in Father. The couple's previous rediscovery of some happiness was not necessarily the beginning of positive growth. While for days at a time Mother thinks she might love her husband as she had before, she realizes that her dream that they would "discover a life of genius" will never happen. She recognizes her own diminishing beauty but sees her husband as "gone dull, made stupid," and having reached his limits; he is very far from genius then. Her contemplation, especially when compared to her husband's in the earlier chapter, is self-centered, lacking in self-awareness, and produces no positive action.

Yet the family members are also happy in their escape. Porters push them around in hired chairs for leisurely rides. Curiously it is Grandfather and his grandson who are not contented to sit back for the ride. The boy would rather hire the chair without the porter so he can do the pushing, and Grandfather while being pushed uses his cane to press people out of his way. Again there is a contrast between the active and passive.

One night the family stops at a pavilion, and they hear one of the songs Walker had played for them. Mother thinks not just of Walker but of her brother. She is struck by "a wave of passionate admiration" for her brother and feels she neglected him. The admiration she wants to have for her husband is transferred to her brother. She can think of her relationship with her brother in terms of her own role as well, not just in the self-centered manner she thinks of her husband and his limitations.

Mother thinks also of the guests at the hotel "waiting for some recognition from her." Again, she is the focus. Various guests are described, and we are startled to learn there are German engineers at the hotel and a German boat examining the coast. "How far off is World War I?" the reader wonders, while Mother and Father notice these events but are not concerned.

Mother is intrigued by a lively foreigner dressed like a movie director. He introduces himself as Baron Ashkenazy and works in the film business. He is an animated man, with the constant habit of raising to his eye a rectangular glass frame that he wears around his neck to frame real-life images. The man's joy of life is infectious, and the family has dinner with him and his daughter. He tells them that his wife has died, that he has made a great deal of money from his first two movies, and that he will make even more from his next one. Mother looks at her son and the baron's beautiful daughter and imagines them as a miniature bride and groom.

In **chapter 34** the reader finds out that the energetic man dressed in the stereotyped film garb is exposed as Tateh. He made money producing dozens of his movie books and then designed a magic lantern, which also sold quite well. He became a partner at the novelty company that bought his books and then sold his portion to enter the movie business. He started calling himself a baron when he saw that such changes helped the daughters of immigrants marry well, and he believed it made it easier for him to be accepted. He also died his hair black again to complete the transformation.

Tateh's daughter and the Little Boy become close companions, spending all of their time together in carefree fun and exploration. One day when it storms they take cover under the boardwalk, and Mother and Tateh start searching for them, she leaning on his arm and he noticing her beauty as the rain wets her dress and hair. They are relieved to find the two children, to the point where Tateh does a somersault, handstand, and cartwheel in delight, all of this occurring as Father sleeps.

Father has become restless at the shore. He sees no easy way for his family to resume their lives outside of Atlantic City. He is sensitive enough to see that his wife feels secure away from New Rochelle, but he knows, too, that she is deluding herself in believing they might only need to go back after the Walker affair is over. At this point, Father reads the newspaper and sees more bad news. Namely, Walker and his cohorts have taken over Morgan's library, and have thrown a grenade in the street in front of it, demanding a negotiation if the authorities want to keep the library and its treasures intact. Soon after reading this, Father receives a phone call from the Manhattan district attorney's office and leaves the shore. It is curious that while in Mother's own mind she has dismissed her husband for having reached his limits, she willingly sends her husband off and takes no part in speaking with the police about Walker. It seems that she may have reached her limit.

Chapter 35 opens with the scene at the library. First the narrator comments that Walker's actions may seem insane, but then he asks, as if to validate the actions, "Or is injustice, once suffered, a mirror universe, with laws of logic and principles of reason the opposite of civilization's?" The authorities again are paralyzed, not willing to take action until they contact Morgan, who is on a ship on the Atlantic. Once again, crowds swarm and police are "everywhere." The police have set up makeshift headquarters across the street from the library. All of the authorities shy away from taking control of the situation and agree on giving that responsibility to the District Attorney of New York, Charles S. Whitman, a man well-known for having prosecuted a police lieutenant and who is seen as a logical candidate for governor or even the U.S. presidency. Whitman obtains the architectural plans of the library and sends a policeman to sneak through the garden and onto the roof to peer inside and determine how many men are in the building. Shortly after the man is sent off, there is an explosion, and all realize that the grounds have been mined.

In **chapter 36** Whitman confers with other authorities and the police. One officer tells him it is best to get an "armed maniac" to talk, since it calms the man down. Whitman immediately goes outside with a megaphone and addresses Walker. A window at the library opens and something is thrown out toward Whitman. Whitman goes back inside, thinking this may be another explosive. But when there is no detonation, Whitman sends a man out to get the item, which turns out to be a rare drinking stein from the seventeenth century with a paper inside with the phone number of the library on it.

Whitman calls the number and is "stunned by the calm businesslike tone of the black man," hardly the maniac Whitman had anticipated. Walker again makes his same demands. Whitman tells him that he cannot hand over Conklin but that he can investigate "the case and see what statutes apply, if any." It is a lame promise, and Walker says he will blow up the library if his demands aren't met in twenty-four hours. He hangs up, leaving Whitman shaken.

Whitman orders Emma Goldman arrested and then contemplates what action is best for him politically. Reporters surround Goldman and she tells them that while it is sad that men have died in this confrontation, Walker's fiancée had a "cruel death" as well. She says of Walker, "I applaud his appropriation of the Morgan property," and adds, for comparison, "Mr. Morgan has done some appropriating of his own.... The oppressor is wealth, my friends." Special editions of the newspapers are published, liberally quoting Goldman and again working against the authorities. Yet the news gains the attention of Booker T. Washington, who, in a speech he gives in New York, deplores Goldman's comments and Walker's actions. Whitman jumps on the opportunity to ask this famous black man to talk to Walker.

In **chapter 37** we learn that Booker T. Washington was the most famous black man in the United States during the time of the Walker confrontation. He is highly respected by many whites as well as blacks and is against the use of violence to solve societal problems. Washington is allowed inside the library, where he sees all its grandeur completely wired with explosives. He is surprised, too, to see a white man painted with a black face and that there are very few men inside. He is quite angry now, and says to Walker, "For my entire life I have worked in patience and hope for a Christian brotherhood. I have had to persuade the white man that he need not fear us or murder us, because we wanted only to improve ourselves and peaceably join him in enjoyment of the fruits of American democracy.... [E]very incident of faulted Negro character has cost me a piece of my life.... What will it cost my students laboring to learn a trade by which they can earn their livelihood and still white criticism!"

Walker responds softly and tells Washington he is honored to meet him and has always admired him. Yet he astonishes Washington when he says, "We might both be servants of our color who insist on the truth of our manhood and the respect it demands." Washington is so disturbed that he starts to lose consciousness and is led to a chair. He observes the excessive riches in the room and begs Walker to leave with him and give himself up, saying he will plead on Walker's behalf for a swift trial and painless execution. Washington then says Walker also should think of his son and all the other black children who will have to struggle through life.

Walker is contemplative. There are tears in his eyes as he says that he wants the fire chief to bring him his automobile completely restored. It is a major concession, since he doesn't ask that Conklin be given to him, yet Washington doesn't see this and instead feels only the rejection of his request.

Based on Washington's report, in **chapter 38**, Whitman orders the evacuation of all dwellings within a two-block radius. At this point Father arrives and upon overhearing the reporters immediately realizes that Walker's demands have been downgraded, although none of the men seem to have noticed. Finally Father comes upon the district attorney and explains his perspective. Whitman is interested but waiting for word from Morgan, which arrives a few moments later. He reads the message and yells at everyone to leave the room except for Father. When everyone is gone, Whitman hands Father the message, which reads, "Give him his automobile and hang him." Whitman, though, is adamant that he cannot go along with this idea, since it would ruin his career if he looks like he is giving in.

Father adds a new twist that makes the idea acceptable to Whitman. He tells Whitman that since Morgan wrote the message, the plan is Morgan's and Whitman is absolved of the responsibility for it. Whitman sees that Father is right and takes action. He orders that Walker's Model T be brought to the front of the library. He phones Walker and proposes that they hash out a plan, with Father being the intermediary. For the first time, Father has "grave misgivings," yet he enters the library, where the first person he sees is his brother-in-law. He is so astonished that, like Booker T. Washington, he must immediately be ushered to a chair.

As Father negotiates back and forth, Whitman sets in motion a manhunt for Conklin, who eventually is brought in, disheveled and scared. Whitman's offer now is that he will talk to the appropriate district attorney about the charges to bring against Conklin, that he will have the fire chief help restore the Model T in front of the library for all to see, and that the car will be completely returned to its original state. In return Whitman wants Walker and his men to give themselves up, and he will guarantee that they are treated properly under the law.

Father relays the message at the library, and Walker tells him he will surrender himself but not the others. Whitman is not happy with the deal, but Father explains the advantages of it and what to tell the newspapers to make the plan agreeable to the public and to save Whitman's political future.

Whitman plans to follow the revolutionaries, rather than just letting them go free. But Walker anticipates this possibility and decides his men will take Father as a hostage to ensure their safe getaway. While Father had been nervous when he entered the library on his first trip, now he is vindictive. He fantasizes about being responsible for the men's eventual capture, feeling "only joy" at the thought of helping to catch his own brother-in-law as well. Whereas the reader may have assumed that Father's earlier self-examination was leading him toward growth, we do not see that here. He certainly is strong, intelligent, and practical, yet these are not new strengths, and his reaction here indicates a destroyed relationship with his brother-in-law and would not endear him towards his wife. Indeed, it seems odd that during the whole time Father has been in New York we read nothing of him contacting his family, another indication of his emotional and psychological distance from them.

In **chapter 39** Conklin, under the direction of two mechanics, suffers through restoring Walker's Model T in the street for all to see. Meanwhile, inside the library, Walker's followers work hard to convince him to change his mind and not stay behind. They feel abandoned and see his decision as "suicide," yet he will not give in and instead sits at Morgan's desk and writes his will. Doom seems imminent.

Father, now a hostage, finally thinking of his wife and wondering what he will tell her about her brother-in-law, decides he should talk to the man. Brother lashes out at Father, saying he could not transmit a message through Father. He accuses Father of paying his employees poorly; of being unaware of their needs; and of being self-delusional, "like all of those who oppress humanity," since Father still believes himself a gentleman. As Younger Brother speaks to Father, the young man is washing up and donning his cuff links, collar, tie, and other items of respectability. Each man wears the same costume of decency, but each views the other as anything but that.

Walker says good-bye to all his men, and tells Father he won't be going with them as hostage after all. There is an ironic twist as Walker says Younger Brother, whose face is now washed back to white, will act as hostage, since all white men look alike anyway. In another twist, Father had told the district attorney earlier that there was one fewer follower than there actually was, inadvertently not counting his brother-in-law in the group. Additionally, Father had never told him that there was a white man painted with a black face in the group. These omissions, then, actually should help the brother-in-law when the police later search for the men, although at that point we assume Father will provide more information. The followers leave the library to get into the restored Model T; Walker sits, holding the plunger of the dynamite detonation box. Father is quite frightened, believes he will die, and sits down, not in a plush armchair but on the floor in a reduced state. There is total stillness, and then Walker asks Father for as many details that he can tell him about his son. This is the end of part three.

Chapter 40 is the only chapter in part four and the last chapter of the book. In accordance with the negotiations, about two hours after the men have driven away in the Model T, Walker leaves the library with his hands up. He is shot repeatedly by lines of police. Later the police say he had tried to escape, but, according to the narrator, "[m]ore probably" Walker had made some small move that he knew would provoke shots and bring about his death.

We are taken to the followers' hideout, where the men are directionless and as of yet unaware of the shooting. They tell Younger Brother he can have the Model T, and that night he takes off and drives as far as he can. He continues driving for some days and then eventually sells the car and wades through the Rio Grande to a town in Mexico that has suffered from numerous occupations by federal troops and insurgents. He is allowed into Zapata's peasant army, when the leader finds out that Brother can create weaponry. The men respect him but see him as reckless, and he eventually loses his life at the same place where Zapata dies years later. This is another coincidence, perhaps pointing to the notion that in death the famous are not so different from the non-famous.

We are reminded that at this time Woodrow Wilson is president, having been chosen by the people "for his qualities as a warrior." We are told that "[t]he signs of the coming conflagration were everywhere," and brace ourselves, since we know, of course, that World War I is on the horizon, but we are unsure how this will affect the characters in this book. J. P. Morgan sees that the royalty in various European nations he visits are greatly disturbed. They are intent on leaving and approach Morgan with numerous pieces they want to sell. Some of the rulers, in desperation, even offer children or wives for sale.

But Morgan is still intent on his Egyptian trip, having decided to find a site along the Nile River where he can have his own pyramid tomb built. He stops at Giza first, insisting on sleeping in the tomb by himself because of his belief that Osiris might reveal to him the state of his soul or physical vitality. Morgan watches for signs through the night but only winds up cold, bitten by bedbugs, and disturbed by a dream in which he is a lowly peddler; all of these he dismisses as not being true signs. Not long after, Morgan dies, knowing he will return to earth in a new form because he is "so urgently needed."

The scene next shifts to Sarajevo, where we expect to experience the death of Archduke Franz Ferdinand. Indeed he is riding through the city and there is a sudden loud noise, much smoke, and loud shouting, but it is from a bomb that someone has thrown that does not cause injury to the archduke and his wife. Furious, the archduke directs his chauffeur to drive them out of the city, and it is here in a side street that the would-be heir to the Austro-Hungarian throne is shot dead.

Few Americans think the circumstance significant when they hear the news, but Houdini ponders it, remembering when he had flown his plane for the archduke, and contemplating the ease with which even a man of power can lose his life to another man. Houdini is performing that day, and we get a lengthy description of his experience as he is tied in a straightjacket and attached to a cable that pulls him up, feet first, above Times Square. As he is pulled to the proper height, everything is upside down and sometimes rotating, quite fitting for a world on the brink of war and for a book wherein fictional characters as well as historical people have recently died, most of them tragically and suddenly.

Houdini "had lately been feeling better about himself." This is due to the fact that in the midst of his personal search for a possible true spiritualist that can connect him to his mother, he is unmasking fraudulent spiritualists. There is some irony here as someone leans out a window and curses at Houdini, who is being watched in awe by the spectators below and who, in fact, can escape from the straightjacket in less than a minute but will do it slower to appear "legitimate." It is when Houdini is upside down that he remembers that the small boy had told him to warn the duke. The statement had been baffling to Houdini at the time, but now he sees it as a message from someone who does have a special connection to the world beyond.

Houdini visits the boy's home, but no one is there since they are on their way, with Mother driving, to the Maine shore. Father and Mother are now hardly speaking and often separated. Father is in Washington, D.C., with plans that Younger Brother had left for him in repayment for Father letting him live in his home and for Father giving him a job. The plans are for advanced military equipment and are so ingenious that Father is in negotiations not only with the United States Army and Navy but with leaders from some

European countries that have been deemed appropriate by the U.S. government. Later Father boards the *Lusitania* to make his first shipments of grenades to London. He contributes to the death of twelve hundred passengers, including himself, since the weapons the ship carries cause extensive explosions that lead to its rapid sinking when it is torpedoed. A fictional character is a participant in a major historical event, again calling into question the nature of history and fiction.

Father is described here as "the immigrant, as in every moment of his life, arriving eternally on the shore of his Self." We have seen already that Father's personality has stayed the same through much of the book, even though he has had chances to start anew. Here the narrator also makes an ironic comment in calling Father an immigrant, the very type of person Father has scorned.

Mother, even though she seems to have no emotion left for her husband, wears black for a year, another indication of her concern about how she is perceived by society. Tateh, who had found out his wife had died, proposes to Mother and finally explains that he is not a baron. She promptly accepts the proposal. Theirs is quite a fairy tale, where the timing of events not only works out well but where the baronly "prince" admits he is not a baron but will still pretend to be and Mother still accepts him. The new family moves to California, and Tateh is inspired by his ethnically diverse children to develop a film about a similarly mixed group of youths who are ragamuffins and have funny adventures as they get into and out of trouble. The idea becomes several movies, not just one. The films are light and ignore prejudice and also the plight of those who are different and/or poor and living in America at the time. Tateh has not just rejected his poor past, then, but has rejected serious art in favor of what sells. The films create an illusion of well-being, just as Tateh has created the illusion of being a baron.

"And by that time," the narrator tells us, "the era of Ragtime had run out, with the heavy breath of the machine, as if history were no more than a tune on a player piano." The war is also over, and this undoubtedly contributes to the feeling of an age having ended and "run out." Loose ends are tied up concerning other more minor characters as well. Goldman is deported; Nesbit is lost in obscurity; and Thaw, released from the insane asylum, now marches annually in the Armistice Day parade. The time of potential change is over, then; the media makers are no more, and even those previously viewed as insane have been absorbed; there is an armistice all around.

PETER F. NEUMEYER ON E.L. DOCTOROW, KLEIST, AND THE ASCENDANCY OF THINGS

One character, for a time, stands out in Doctorow's *Ragtime*— the mysterious, willful, foppish "upstart" Negro, Coalhouse Walker Jr. (The cognate Kohlhaas/Coalhouse needs no further explanation. Consider, though, that the German Kohlhaas can be transliterated, *Kohl* = *Kohle* = coal, and *haas* = *Haas*(?) = hatred).

Without my retelling Doctorow's intricate story, note that Coalhouse Walker Jr. drives his pride, his most precious jewel, his black Model T Ford, as is his wont, past the Emerald Isle Volunteer Fire Company on his way from Westchester to New York. Further note that, in precise parallel to the story of Michael Kohlhaas, the bullying Chief of the Volunteer Fire Dept., at first half in jest perhaps, then in all earnestness, halts Coalhouse and his Model T, demanding a twenty-five dollar toll which, though it "had never before been collected ... was nevertheless in force." Coalhouse tries to back out, finds himself boxed in, abandons his car, seeks official help, having left (like Kohlhaas) someone to watch the car, fails to get help, returns to find the watchers gone, the car in a field, mud-bespattered, with a six-inch tear in the pantasote top, and a mound of fresh human excrement in the back seat.

The Kohlhaas/Coalhouse parallel holds precisely for the rest of the story, the latter's fiancée dying as a consequence of the evolving disaster in which Coalhouse gathers to himself a band of loyal followers. Coalhouse transfers his personal meticulousness and property to an inflexible and insatiable quest for justice, terrorizing Westchester communities, setting fire to fire houses, calling out the original offending Volunteer Fire Company with a false alarm and, as the men come into the street, blasting them with shotgun. Considerable attention is paid in the narration to the description of the fire company horses, evoking, of course, further recollections of the horses in

Kleist's story. In the end, Coalhouse and his followers barricade themselves into the great art depository that is the J. Pierpont Morgan library, on 36th street. They will blow up the entire collection, the entire building, unless restitution is made, and Coalhouse's Model T is returned in its original condition. Bully-boy fire chief Will Conklin is publicly humiliated by having to repair the car in the middle of the street, Coalhouse's followers are given assurances of safe conduct out, Coalhouse exits, and is executed by a waiting police firing squad as he walks with his hands up out into the middle of 36th street.

Perusal of the ingenious parallel of Doctorow's fascinating tale with its source leads to speculation about the differing significance of Kleist's novella and Doctorow's magic lantern show.

Kleist's character, Kohlhaas, is in the tradition of Coriolanus and of Ahab—obsessive, monomaniacal, infinitely grander than life in his singleness of purpose. Kleist's story is named *Michael Kohlhaas*. The story is the tragedy of Michael Kohlhaas, solely, and his particular fall is the concern. When he is ended, the story is ended. I use the word "tragedy" in a strict sense, for Kleist's is in fact the story of the fall of a great man, a great man in precisely the Aristotelian sense. The fall is from a very high station because of a personal characteristic of the hero. It is the characteristic that has accounted, when unobstructed, for the grandeur of Caesar and Moses. When this same drive which has led to greatness in some, has become blocked or frustrated in others, it manifests itself in the frenzy of a Coriolanus, a Quixote, a Kohlhaas.

On the other hand, Doctorow's Coalhouse is, though perhaps the most memorable character, still only one of the passing parade of foolish mortals shuffling through *Ragtime*. Whom do we not see in Doctorow's novel? Houdini, President McKinley, J. Pierpont Morgan, Henry Ford, Emma Goldman—their progress is lit for a moment only, till each passes into the shadows to make way for the next character. The novel is a panoply of historical or fictional or ficto-historical characters in real events, in made-up events, in half-made-up-events—we never know for sure. And it doesn't matter really, for it all passes phantasmagorically. Moving pictures are a leitmotif of the novel, and moving pictures are nothing but shadows of reality. These shadows of reality, Doctorow seems to suggest, are emblematic of the time itself, shadow pictures always in flux, never graspable, and essentially as unreconstructable as those earlier, and by no means simpler, decades of our century.

Doctorow's Coalhouse is not central to the book. He is merely one character in it—and he comes to naught—his small raggedy band of pre-Symbionese Liberation Army militia, with a white man ("Mother's Younger Brother") joining them in blackface, disappearing into nowhere or everywhere.

The center of gravity in the novel is not any one person. *Ragtime's* center of gravity is in things, and the prime-movers of the tale are the makers of things, the financers of things, the inventors of things. As the cause of Coalhouse's rage, war, and execution is the most American thing there is—the car, the Model T—so the semi-seen movers of the tale, the *eminence grises* are Henry Ford, the perfecter of the things, and J.P. Morgan, the underwriter of a world of chattel.

(...)

The answer to the original question seems clear. Destruction of the J. P. Morgan collection, crazy, eclectic, and ill-gotten symbol of the material and pyramidal worship of our own bandit Pharaoh, would be the day of our locusts, our armageddon. But the repair of the Model T saves us and paves the way for the salvation of modern America as we like it. The N.Y.C.P.D. exterminates the closest modern approximation to a tragic hero, Coalhouse Walker, with the diminutive "Jr." appended to his name.

Not for horses, mind you, but for a Model T. Not flesh and blood, but a machine—with shit on the seat.

Coalhouse is not a minor actor; he does strut; he does fret, and he has, indeed, his poor hour. He is not destitute, for he is a strong-spirited man, a reaffirmation of will incarnate, though perhaps somewhat ludicrous in his costume, in his questionable posturings. Still—and this is the point—Coalhouse is no Kohlhaas. Coriolanus appears in *Coriolanus*, Othello in *Othello*, and even Quixote, a hero manque, has his novel named for him. But Coalhouse, significantly, is only one shadowy presence out of many on the *Ragtime* silver screen. As much as to say, "he's not much of a hero. But he's all the hero we got." He causes only a ripple, and that only when he threatens to blow up things.

Except you have the power of things or guns, the novel seems to say, you are as interchangeable as is one Model T radiator with another, and your essence is not even as real as the hundreds of silhouettes snipped out of paper by Doctorow's character, Tateh. You are as evanescent, and of substance as questionable as the cinema shadows that same character produces when, at novel's end he's in the cinema serials game, "in partnership with the Pathé exchange."

BARBARA FOLEY ON THE FORMS OF HISTORICAL CONSCIOUSNESS IN MODERN FICTION

Doctorow himself has been most explicit about his sense of alienation from the school of "documentary" writers (who have also been called "new journalists" and "nonfiction novelists"). His plan in *Ragtime*, he states, is to "deify" facts: "give 'em all sorts of facts—made up facts, distorted facts. It's the reverse of Truman Capote. I see all these new journalists as guys on the other side."[35] Pursuing the epistemological implications of this practice, he has remarked that he is currently testing the proposition that

> there's no more fiction or nonfiction now, there's only narrative. All the nonfiction means of communication employ narrative today. Television news is packaged using devices of drama and suspense and image. News-magazines package fact as fiction—in the sense of organizing and composing the material esthetically. There's something else: the reader of a novel usually

thinks, well, these things really happened to the author, but for legal or other reasons he's changed everybody's name. In 'Ragtime' I've just twisted that around and written about imaginary events in the lives of undisguised people.[36]

In fundamental outlook, however, Doctorow may not be as distant from Capote as he believes. Georg Lukács, discussing the writer's alienation from history in the modern period, has observed that, once the writer loses faith in the direction of history, it either becomes "a collection and reproduction of interesting facts about the past" or "a chaos to be ordered as one likes."[37] David Lodge draws a similar conclusion from his analysis of contemporary fiction:

> *The Armies of the Night* and *Giles Goatboy* are equally products of the apocalyptic imagination. The assumption behind such experiments is that our 'reality' is so extraordinary, horrific or absurd that the methods of conventional realistic imitation are no longer adequate.... Art can no longer compete with life on equal terms, showing the universal in the particular. The alternatives are either to cleave to the particular—to 'tell it like it is'— or to abandon history altogether and construct pure fictions which reflect in an emotional or metaphorical way the discords of contemporary experience.[38]

The imagination which conceives Houdini as "the last of the great shameless mother-lovers" (p. 30) is, perhaps, subtly allied with that which insists that Robert Lowell was on the steps of the Lincoln Memorial in the fall of 1967: both, in Doctorow's words, "deify" facts—the principal difference being that Mailer displays the journalist's reverence for facts which are externally verifiable, while Doctorow pays equal homage to facts corroborated in the historical record and those which are the products of his own imagination.

It is, however, with the contemporary school of "apocalyptic" historical novelists—whom Mas'ud Zavarzadeh, in his recent

The Mythopoeic Reality, would dub "transfictionists"[39]—that Doctorow has a closer affinity. To group under this single rubric such diverse writers as Barth, Fowles, Pynchon, Berger, García Márquez, and Doctorow is, of course, a problematic enterprise. First, as Martin Green has pointed out, Berger, Fowles, and Doctorow actually belong to a subgenre within this grouping, whose distinguishing characteristic is, in addition to elegance, taste, tact, and erudition, a penchant for "teas[ing] ... the reader ... to discover the imaginative status of [their] characters and events—the status and character of the imaginative experience he is being offered."[40] Second, it is questionable whether a writer like Pynchon can be said to be "apocalyptic" in *Gravity's Rainbow* in exactly the same way that he is in *V.*: in Pynchon and other contemporary novelists, the 1970's may be witnessing a somewhat different version of the "apocalyptic" outlook of the decade before. Nonetheless, what the various writers of this tendency have in common is a fundamental skepticism about the "objective" nature of historical reality—or, to put it another way, about the necessary subjectivity which any writer infuses into his attempt to reconstruct a picture of the past. Aware that distortions of "history" have often been legitimated in the name of objectivity, writers like Berger and García Márquez are openly challenging the positivist view of history: hence the patent mysticism of Melquiades's prophecy to the unchanged generations in *One Hundred Years of Solitude*, and the equally mystical process by which G. discovers a rationale for committed political action in the present through reversion to memories of senseless violence buried deep in his subconscious mind.

In one sense what such novelists are confronting is an epistemological problem which has been familiar to practicing historians and philosophers of history for some time: the crucial distinction between what Charles Beard called "history as past actuality" and "history as thought."[41] In another sense, however, the pronounced historical self-consciousness of a Fowles or a Barth significantly corresponds to the historicist tendency of much post–World War II historical writing, which projects a keen awareness of the historian's inbuilt bias and tends to shun the positivist application of general "covering laws" to a given series of historical particulars.[42] Doctorow's bold grafting of fictional invention onto the historical experience of a Houdini or a Goldman is curiously related to Collingwood's definition of history as a "web of imaginative construction":[43] implicit in both is an open acknowledgement of the process of selection—indeed, of creation—which is inherent in the task of the historical writer. Like Tom Stoppard in *Travesties* or Nicholas Meyer in *The Seven-Per-Cent Solution*, Doctorow wants not only to entertain his audience with audacious historical improbabilities but also deliberately to carry the process of historical "creation" to the threshold of fantasy. "One of the governing ideas of this book," he has declared, "is that facts are as much of an illusion as anything else."[44]

Notes

35. Gussow, p. 12. In the original version, the article read "defy" facts. This error was corrected, however, in the next day's edition of the *Times*.

36. Clemens, p. 76.

37. Lukács, pp. 176, 181.

38. David Lodge, "The Novelist at the Crossroads," in *The Novelist at the Crossroads and Other Essays on Fiction and Criticism* (Ithaca, N.Y., 1971), p. 33.

39. Zavarzadeh, pp. 38–41.

40. Martin Green, "Nostalgia Politics," *American Scholar*, XLV (Winter, 1975–1976), 841.

41. Charles Beard, "Written History as an Act of Faith," *American Historical Review*, XXXIX (Jan. 1934), 219; rpt. in Hans Meyerhoff, ed., *The Philosophy of History in Our Time: An Anthology* (Garden City, N.Y., 1959), p. 140.

42. For a stimulating account of the relationship between contemporary historicism and the "apocalyptic" novel—especially V.—see Mark A. Weinstein, "The Creative Imagination in Fiction and History," *Genre*, IX (Summer, 1976), 263–277.

43. R.G. Collingwood, *The Idea of History* (1946; rpt. London, 1967), p. 242.

44. Quoted in Donelson, p. 22.

Ragtime (1975) is like those musical comedy entertainments turned out by MGM and RKO in the 1930s, with Busby Berkeley settings, and perhaps held together by Fred Astaire or Gene Kelly a little later. Such entertainments had a story line that existed solely as cement for the musical numbers, dance sequence, or spectaculars. They had, in a sense, some linkage to circuses, to Barnum & Bailey's three rings. Such entertainments catered to nearly all tastes, since if one number bombed, there was quickly another. *Ragtime* is of this kind, the narrative serving as a kind of glue for all the sideshows: Houdini, J.P. Morgan, Henry Ford, Evelyn Nesbit, Stanford White and Harry Thaw, Emma Goldman, Henry Clay Frick.

Some of the "headliners" remain on stage through much of the novel, but most do their act and then depart: Freud, Zapata, Ford, and a few others. Also, there are brief scenes between some of the characters who never met in actuality, and whose relationship is not, of course, developed beyond the meeting itself. Evelyn Nesbit and Emma Goldman, for example, have a sexually charged scene together, as Emma, the political firebrand, rubs down Evelyn, the kept woman of rich and half-crazy men.

To hold the circus together, Doctorow uses an intense social and political sense, an irreverent view of the American past, updated to justify contemporary cynicism. Morgan is the most powerful man in the world, but his real interest lies in eternal life and transcendence, like the ancient pharaohs of Egypt. Unable to settle only for power now, he needs assurance that it will not all be dissipated after death. Opposite him is Henry Ford, intent on consolidating what he has, uninterested in the afterlife, and satisfied by reading a twenty-five-cent copy of *An Eastern Fakir's Eternal Wisdom*. There, he finds a simple explanation of reincarnation. "I explain my genius this way— some of us have just lived more times than others.... And I'll tell you something in thanks for the eats, I'm going to lend that book to you." To which Morgan rejoins: "Mr. Ford ... if my ideas can survive their ultimate attachment to you, they will have met their ultimate test."

Much of the book is set within that parodic frame of reference, although not all. Harry Houdini runs through the entire length of the narrative, and he is, like Daniel in *The Book of Daniel*, a poignant figure. In his legend, Houdini creates the semblance of conquering man's destiny. But Doctorow's Houdini is a deeply obsessed man who knows all his feats are tricks, aware none of them is connected to the real world. He, Houdini, must create an artificial situation, which he can then overcome; his feats, accordingly, are heroic solely as reflections, not as realities. He is obsessed with creating greater tricks, confronting death as a way of forcing the reality which eludes him. Houdini competes with gods, and yet life restrains him from that ultimate transcendence of himself.

(...)

Black rights are born amidst terror and destruction, and of course, the violent death of the leader, Walker. Younger Brother drifts off to join the Mexican revolution, and is killed. Morgan dies, convinced he has perceived the signs that he will be called back on earth, especially since he foresees a war coming, and a war without Morgan would be unthinkable. Freud returns to Europe, certain that America is a second-rate civilization. Houdini dies and is reborn, dies once more, is reborn, but is still unable to respond to the real situation, being doomed to react only to his own devices. Evelyn Nesbit, after having driven men mad with her seductiveness, loses her looks and drifts into anonymity. Political activity becomes increasingly senseless as the world drifts into a war; one of the final scenes shows a Serbian national at Sarajevo.

Like a ragtime musical bit, the novel turns on its variations. It is a light but expert job, with the sound of Scott Joplin tinkling through episodes and variations, always returning to the same rhythms and undertones. History is everyone's destiny, Morgan and Walker alike. Only acquisitions differ, Morgan with his wealthy artifacts, Walker with his beloved

Model T. The individual life, consumed by goods, rolls on. This is hardly profound, but history is like ragtime, full of variations on certain common assumptions about mankind, and just about as certain.

Ragtime, like *Loon Lake*, five years later, is Doctorow's effort to discover another beat or tone to American life. The novel as musical comedy, lightly parodic, an entertainment: these are his adaptations. They are, apparently, ways of responding to the sixties, modes that assimilate music, television, film, the stage, on which famous people perform.

Notes

1. "lend that book to you": *Ragtime* (1975; London: Pan, 1976), p. 174.

2. "their ultimate test": Ibid., p. 175.

GEOFFREY GALT HARPHAM ON E.L. DOCTOROW AND THE TECHNOLOGY OF NARRATIVE

This chain of related concepts—transformation, volatility, repetition, durability, replication—defines what might be called simply "the process," whose effects *Ragtime* traces everywhere, just as Daniel traced the secret circuitry of his world. The process achieves visibility in all the characters: in Evelyn Nesbit, a figure of pure replicability as a Floradora girl, a model for a statue, a media celebrity, and a movie star; in Tateh, who begins by making silhouettes, then develops flipbooks of primitive "animation," and ends as a motion picture director; in Emma Goldman, whose politics are based on collectivism and revolution—duplication and volatility; in Coalhouse Walker, who becomes a political force when his followers adopt the collective name "Coalhouse," becoming representations of him. The Model T on whose uniqueness he paradoxically insists is actually a case of duplication so utter that there cannot even be said to be an original. Even figures such as Mother and Father are figural, replicated by other mothers and fathers in the story. Everything that makes *Ragtime* unusual as a narrative—including the unplaceability of its narrative voice, its numerous replications and parallelisms of character and incident, its undefinable ontology, being at once diary, journalism, realistic novel, and history—contributes to a deemphasis of particularities and to a corresponding emphasis on the common destiny of the entire era. Everything is symptomatic of the process, an instance of it; everything is presented in miniature and has the curiously aesthetic quality of tiny things.

Miniaturization notwithstanding, *Ragtime* is a work of great aspiration, a sustained meditation in the form of a group conversation seen from above, on the subjects of mutability, human identity, the relation of the individual to the social and political collectivity. And, again and again, on the subject of technology. In a conversation with Henry Ford, J. P. Morgan suggests that the true brilliance of the assembly line is that it repeats and confirms "an organic truth," the principle that "the interchangeability of parts is a rule of nature." "Shared design," according to Morgan, "is what allows taxonomists to classify mammals as mammals. And within a species—man, for example—the rules of nature operate so that our individual differences occur on the basis of our similarity" (122). Morgan is describing Doctorow's methods as well as Ford's, for *Ragtime* gives the appearance of having been produced by a narratological assembly line. Doctorow has said that his primary consideration while composing was "relentless pace";[5] and to maintain the pace he has not only eliminated most description, "setting," and "background" but also effaced the differences between the various elements of his narrative— between large and small, speech and thought, speech and description, historically real and fictional characters. These superfluities and inconvenient singularities have suffered the fate of the individuality of the assembly-line worker—they have been sacrificed in the interests of efficiency.

Continuing the project of *The Book of Daniel*, *Ragtime* posits a master principle—the process—uniting all elements of theme and technique, a principle so comprehensive that it even accounts for the production of the narrative itself. But *Ragtime* also marks a new sensitivity to what might be called the requirements for success. If compared to its predecessor the novel seems trivial and even vulgar, the reason may be that Doctorow's vision now has room for the happy ending, a fate most conspicuously enjoyed by Mother and Tateh. What segregates them from others is their "capacity to forfeit portions of themselves," to relinquish imaginative projections, to embrace the volatility of the world, and to control their lives by generating successive self-representations. In treating their selves as subject to recomposition, they achieve individuation by mastering the processes of replication.[6]

Father, by contrast, is unable to end, and the boy describes him as a perpetual beginner, "the immigrant, as in every moment of his life, arriving eternally on the shore of his Self" (269). The most poignant example of the incapacity to regard the self as subject to invention and reinvention is Houdini, for whom "the real world" is a stage for tricks "he couldn't touch" (82). After his mother's death, his acts become all too real, and the crowds beg him to stop before he kills himself. "Every feat enacted Houdini's desire for his dead mother. He was buried and reborn, buried and reborn" (170). One of a kind, Houdini is driven by a reverence for the uniqueness of his mother and for the reality of the world, but his insistence on these qualities constitutes a blindness to the force of replication in life. Fittingly, he is condemned to ceaseless repetition and to a rancid fictiveness, unable "to distinguish his life from his tricks" (171). He epitomizes failure in *Ragtime* as an inability to forfeit a portion of oneself, to peel the image off and begin the composition anew.

The most successful character is, finally, the young boy, who materializes miraculously at the very end as an older narrator. He has mingled his memories with popular clichés, historical reconstructions, and invention in a narrative that simultaneously represents the era and falsifies it. This falsification is not, however, an avoidable betrayal of reality, as Fredric Jameson argues in a recent article; for as the text shows, the era was never fully present to itself: it constantly produced effects it could neither control nor predict and so was always becoming known and unknown to itself. This narrative does not render the essence of the era but arranges those parts of it that were forfeited or left behind. Including himself in his narrative, the narrator accepts the fact that falsification, distance, and "the process" affect self-knowledge as well as historical knowledge.

Notes

5. "What I set out to do in *Ragtime* was compose a narrative that moved at an absolutely relentless pace" ("*Ragtime*" 7). In this interview Doctorow also reveals that he composed the novel in assembly-line fashion, perfecting each page in its turn and adding it to the rest.

6. Doctorow is extremely interested in the "parts" of the human personality. In "False Documents" he claims that modern psychology—with its concepts of "complex," "sublimation," "repression," "identity crisis," "object relations," "borderline," and so on—"is the industrialization of story-telling" (231). But in "The Language of Theater" he describes "the disciplines of social science, whose case studies, personality typing and composite social portraiture are the industrialized forms of storytelling" (638).

EMILY MILLER BUDICK ON E.L. DOCTOROW'S *RAGTIME* AND THE MORAL FICTION OF HISTORY

Ford's restatement of Morgan's philosophy exposes the historiography of reincarnation as a fantasy of the supreme and immortal self escaping reality into its own distorted and sterile delusions.

This is also what Houdini, who is the occasion of the book's opening fantasy, reveals. Houdini understands the finality of death and change. He has gone "all over the world accepting all kinds of bondage and escaping. He was roped to a chair. He escaped. He was chained to a ladder. He escaped.... He escaped ... He escaped ... He escaped. He was buried alive in a grave and could not escape, and had to be rescued. Hurriedly, they dug him out. The earth is too heavy, he said gasping" (pp. 7–8;

cf. p. 227). Nonetheless Houdini is obsessed with the idea of resurrection. He forgets the finality of death and attempts, with literalistic absurdity, to resurrect his dead mother. The remembrance stones he leaves on his mother's gravestone begin to form their own "kind of pyramid." His professional life becomes a grotesque effort to realize the same old Egyptian secrets of immortality and resurrection that obsess Morgan and Ford. Desperately he attempts to actualize the possibilities of rebirth. He is "buried and reborn, buried and reborn" (p. 234) in a painful parody of resurrection.

The blast from the firehouse station down the block from the theater in which Houdini is performing, which sends his terrified audience scurrying from his performance, points to the difference between real life and Houdini's maddening inability to "distinguish his life from his tricks" (p. 234). His efforts to reincarnate himself or his mother represent a childish indulgence. The moment Coalhouse Walker's real grievances burst on the scene, Houdini's trivializing escapist magic loses the affection of his audience (p. 239). Indeed, the Jewish Erich Weiss ought to have intuited the terrible inappropriateness of the Egyptian world of pyramids and pharaohs and eternal life to the people of the promised land. The nature of the American obsession with Egypt, apparently so quaint and harmless as to manifest itself in wallpaper and drapes, is revealed in the young boy's fantasy, wherein Sarah is a "Nubian princess now captured for a slave" (p. 178). No wonder an "unseasonably warm breeze" with a "breath of menace" blows the "window curtain in the Egyptian dining room" (p. 213) while Walker voices his complaint against the white fire chief, and the family advises him to walk away from it. Escape from bondage and the acquisition of the promised land were important to American blacks, as they had been to Jews during the escape from slavery in Egypt. Set in the heartland of America's pharaonic fantasy—Pierpont Morgan's Manhattan estate—Booker T. Washington's prayer, "Oh Lord ... lead my people to the Promised Land. Take them from under the Pharaoh's whip" (p. 327) can only reverberate, like the Negro spiritual in *Go Down, Moses*, with painful irony. Enslavement, whether of blacks or of immigrants or of women, has become an American way of life. America plays a dangerous game when it resurrects Egypt in the promised land. The third part of the book, which follows fast and heavy on the heels of Coalhouse Walker's revenge, unmasks the awful fallacies of the reincarnationist philosophy and the dangers of America's infantile indulgence in it.

The painful violence of Coalhouse Walker's revenge shatters the world of fantasy in which the majority of the characters exist. But Walker's raw, unmitigated realism does no more than reinstate the essential confusion between fantasy and history in reverse. Walker demands that white society "restore" what has been taken from him (p. 212). "I want the infamous Fire Chief of the Volunteers turned over to my justice.... I want my automobile returned to me in its original condition" (p. 243). But changing the possessors of power does not change the principles of power and its corruption.

(...)

Like the Giant fool (p. 267), who misunderstands the rules of the social game, Coalhouse Walker, in a tradition of black activism anticipated by Faulkner's *Go Down, Moses*, unwittingly reproduces the structure of thought that has disenfranchised and mocked him. Coalhouse Walker's violence fails because, like so much else in the book, it ignores the irreversibility of history. It reflects a private vendetta conceptualized wholly in terms of self. He wants his car returned as it was. Walker does not manage to link his vision of personal justice to larger social claims and aspirations. He does not comprehend what will essentially distinguish the black power movement of the sixties. This is the movement toward the celebration of ethnic separateness and difference, which, like Tateh's movies or like the ragtime music Walker plays but doesn't understand, will transform American social structure. Coalhouse Walker is not, as some critics have charged, an anachronistic relocation of the black power movement. He replicates a stage of social thought as yet incapable of dislodging social conservatism in America.

Like Father, Ford, Morgan, Houdini, and other characters in the book, Coalhouse Walker is still seeking the shores of self; like the maps and diagrams, baseball and ice-skating and silhouetting that show social conformity, he can imagine only a single game plan, different only in that it puts him, and not someone else, at the center. Reincarnation and the interchangeability of parts are Morgan's and Ford's philosophies of social oppression. Even the ragtime pianist Walker plays their tune.

MARSHALL BRUCE GENTRY ON *RAGTIME* AS AUTO BIOGRAPHY

I would like to suggest that Coalhouse Walker grows into his individuality, that it is precisely when Mother's Younger Brother is astonished to see Walker equating a mere car with justice (337) that Walker has achieved heroism. It is crucial to the novel that Coalhouse Walker Jr. receives a car that is indeed a duplicate of his original Model T with the PANTASOTE top and at the same time a different car. Surely the car is more significant in its replacement form because the whole of New York's political establishment is watching it. The remade car is also different from the original in the sense that it is *not* produced by assembly line: "Fire Chief Conklin ... piece by piece dismantled the Ford and made a new Ford from the chassis up" (341). One might wonder whether Doctorow is claiming that this car produced by an individual is in some sense morally superior, or whether Doctorow is arguing for a return to the individual craftsman, and my answer would be yes but also no—it is impossible (following a logic that the novel suggests) to have individual craftsmanship, because Willie Conklin becomes the mass of society, "so ordinary as to be like all men," and, at least while he is building the car, he "become[s] Pierpont Morgan, the most important individual of his time" (311). Even as Coalhouse Walker's demand is met, another Model T comes out of mass production. At the same time, it is worth noting that if a Ford cannot be produced by only one individual, not even Henry Ford can make a Ford by himself. The view that presents the Model T as a product of the entire society frees the automobile from Ford's tyranny to some extent. And there is something of a victory for Coalhouse even as the police equate him with the replaced car, complete with what might be considered the symbolically crucial customizing PANTASOTE top. He exchanges his life for the car and for the lives of his band of revolutionaries, all in a sense duplicates of Walker who call themselves Coalhouse.

The issues of the establishment of selfhood in a world of mass production are spelled out even more complexly in the story of the narrator, the Little Boy. *Ragtime* claims, through the Little Boy as narrator, that it is essential that one perceive (and maintain) the differences within apparent duplicates, as well as the similarities in things that seem chaotically dissimilar. Chapter 15 is crucial to an understanding of the Little Boy's fondness both for change, as taught by his grandfather (132–33), and for pattern. Not enough has been said critically about the significance for the boy of minor changes within pattern, of the rare occasion when the hairbrush or window does not remain still (133), of the slight changes that prove "even statues did not remain the same" (134). The Little Boy seems to understand that the slight difference within sameness is the metaphor for his own individuality. Much has been made of the Little Boy's fondness for baseball because, he says, "The same thing happens over and over" (266). According to Barbara L. Estrin, among others, baseball is a prime example of the sameness that rather depressingly underlies the appearance of change (23). But even here we see some delight in novelty, for as soon as the Little Boy praises the pattern, he is excited by the unusual occurrence of a foul ball that ends up in his hands (266–67). The point surely is that the Little Boy can always see both sides, and therein lies his power. Much has been said about the boy's vision of a "macrocephalic image of himself" in Houdini's headlight (11) as a sign that the Little Boy is overly subjective, and some readers have been troubled by such a possibility. Barbara Foley criticizes *Ragtime* for implying that historical meaning as produced by this narrator is "chimerical and at best highly subjective," based on the notion "that whatever coherence emerges from the represented historical world is attributable to the writer's power as teller of his story" (175). The Little Boy's amazing and initially obscure advice for Houdini, that he warn the Archduke Ferdinand of his coming assassination and of WWI, may even seem significant primarily for its pointlessness. In Estrin's interesting reading, the Little Boy's warning in the first chapter is a sort of failed authorial intrusion demonstrating the power of the machine over us all:

> With the insight he gains from subsequent experience, the little boy, prefiguring the storyteller he later becomes, informs the magician. We live our lives in the illusion that we can change things, in the hope that we amount to more than insignificant parts of a vast machine moving inexorably toward doom. The child anticipates, simultaneously as the narrator reconstructs, history.... "Warn the Duke," he says, sounding a command that might alter the course of the novel we are about to read. (19)

Although I do not agree with Barbara Cooper's description of the narrative persona of *Ragtime* as "anonymous," I agree with her idea that the narrator "transcends the limitations of a single human perspective" (8). I would like to emphasize the idea that the narrator's ability to combine points of view is more nearly the ground of his selfhood than a dilution of it. The narrator is at once a product of his time and an individual exercising some effect upon his time. His visions are not all of the sort that ends the first chapter and that Houdini somewhat pathetically reproduces near the novel's end (365). More should be made of the fact that the Little Boy's eyes are compared to a "school globe" (104) and of the line in the description of Sarah's funeral that insists emphatically that the boy sees not just himself but the rest of this society: Sarah's hearse "was so highly polished the boy could see in its rear doors a reflection of the entire street" (223). This line suggests that the Little Boy's visions are at once internal and external.

Note

1. Page references to the text of *Ragtime* are from the mass-produced Bantam paperback edition.

Cushing Strout on Twain, Doctorow, and the Anachronistic Adventures of the Arms Mechanic and the Jazz Pianist

Ragtime was advertised in its jacket copy as a sport: "You will never have read anything like *Ragtime* before. Nothing quite like it has ever been written before." But, in some important respects, it has at least one unnoticed classic American precursor as a speculative and satirical history: Mark Twain's *The Connecticut Yankee in King Arthur's Court* (1889). Like Twain's romance (three times made into a movie), *Ragtime* is also a time-travel story with a deliberate anachronism built into its structure, with a magician playing an important part in the plot, and with an ironic and violent climax involving military technology.

The analogy between these two comic historical romances may seem implausible. Twain's story, unlike Doctorow's, which is told by an imitation of an impersonal historian's narrating voice, is a vernacular, first-person narrative, and its material is legendary, the Arthurian Camelot, far removed from the author's own time and country, unlike Doctorow's prewar period of America. Moreover, the plot of *Ragtime* turns centrally on racial conflict, which is absent from Twain's sixth-century Britain. Yet, the more each text is read over the shoulder of the other, the more interesting correspondences do appear. Are they accidental or was Doctorow, at some level of his mind, aware of Twain's story, which he never mentions in connection with *Ragtime*? At any rate, the audience for Ragtime eagerly assimilated its deceptively simple declarative sentences without paying any attention to its epigraph, a warning by Scott Joplin: "It is never right to play Ragtime fast." A good way to play it slowly is to read the novel side by side with Twain's story. If *The Connecticut Yankee* is not a close relative of *Ragtime*, it is surely at least a first cousin once removed.

(...)

Both Twain and Doctorow by their technique of deliberate anachronism put two eras into juxtaposition. In both books, the later one judges the earlier one. Twain's preface tips his hand, signaling his critique of the Arthurian era, by explaining that if he refers to any laws or customs that did not actually exist in the sixth century, "one is quite justified in inferring that whatever one of these laws or customs was lacking in that remote time, its place was competently filled by a worse one."[9] Doctorow is moved by a similar political indignation to subvert any sentimental nostalgia for the earlier era. He begins with the mock-historical tone of a social historian: "Patriotism was a reliable sentiment in the early 1900's." Then he shifts gears: "There were no Negroes. There were no immigrants.... Across America sex and death were barely distinguishable." The mention of Emma Goldman, the revolutionary anarchist, an immigrant Jew, leads him to this second thought: "Apparently there were Negroes. There were immigrants."[10] The end of chapter 6 coldly enumerates with cumulative force the oppressions suffered by miners, child workers, immigrants, and blacks, while trusts proliferate and the rich entertain themselves by playing at being poor.

Both authors underline the continuity as well as the differences in their comparison of earlier with later times. Twain's treatment of serfdom explicitly insists on its continuity with slavery in the Old South and the old regime in France. By dramatizing the racial conflict of the ragtime era through the takeover of the Morgan Library, a tactic characteristic of radical politics in the 1960s, Doctorow underlines the persistence of racial injustice. More subtly, when the conservative black leader Booker T. Washington encounters the militant Coalhouse Walker in the library, the narrator notes on the wall portraits of Martin Luther, and Washington prays that the Lord may lead his people to the promised land—a strong echo of Martin Luther King, Jr., with Walker playing the role of the radical Malcolm X.[11] Walker's supporters speak in revolutionary terms of setting up a provisional American government. At the same time the story dramatizes another aspect of the 1960s, the reluctance of the authorities to enter into, or respect, negotiations with the rebels.

What saves both books from historical smugness is their refusal to follow a traditional Whig interpretation of history with its idea of progress that congratulates the past for having led to the present. Twain judges the British past by his endorsement of the American and French revolutions. But from this point of view, his present is also criticized. When the Round Table becomes a stock exchange, wildcat manipulations (with which Twain as a heavy investor in the market was familiar) lead to warfare among the knights and the end of the Boss's new deal. He may think that his anomalous position in the kingdom makes him "a giant among pygmies, a man among children, a master intelligence among intellectual moles; by all rational measurement the one and only actually great man in that whole British world."[12] But the reader is made increasingly aware of the dark side of the Boss's project with its complacency about his own assumption of power and his addiction to a technocratic "progress" that depends heavily on weapons of destruction. His political and cultural imperialism is the other side of his role as the democratic reformer.

Notes

9. Mark Twain, *A Connecticut Yankee in King Arthur's Court* (New York: Modern Library, 1949), Preface.

10. *Ragtime*, 3–5.

11. Ibid., 238.

12. *Connecticut Yankee*, 63, 66.

The uncompromising Coalhouse Walker dies for his convictions. Tateh discovers how an entrepreneur can make it in America. Is this compromise a sellout? Or does it suggest a way of social transformation that is more effective than collective revolutionary action? Like Daniel, Tateh becomes a self-progenitor, he creates himself by becoming Baron Ashkenazy the successful filmmaker. "His whole personality had turned outward and he had become a voluble and energetic man full of the future. He felt he deserved his happiness. He'd constructed it without help" (pp. 299–300). Thus, Tateh's discovery of the motion picture, and his abandonment of the static, essentially premodern silhouette, aligns him with the truly modern metamorphosing energies of the twentieth century. The movies show volatility within frames and offer people a vision of difference and otherness, and hence the chance to understand themselves. Both ragtime music and movies are democratizing forces in American culture. As Budick says, "They provide what static and stabilizing images cannot, the possibility for sympathetic self-divestment and identification with the other."[21] The marriage of Tateh and Mother at the end represents a new historical composition, which points to a pluralistic American future, and is perhaps the only composition worthy of survival. What image of our future will or can survive the catastrophe of the Great War? It is Tateh's idea for a series of films about an interracial group of children—like the Our Gang comedies—who get into and out of trouble. It is this vision that offers an alternative to the view of history as a machine, "as if history were no more than a tune on a player piano" (p. 369). Moreover, such a vision is regenerative and morally responsible.

In one sense, Ragtime is about the death of the father, of patriarchy, at least of a certain kind. By the same token, it signals the emergence of woman into the new equation of the twentieth century. The voice and influence of Emma Goldman is strong throughout the novel, speaking for the freedom of women from physical and economic and political servitude. Evelyn Nesbit comes under her care and influence. Even Mother has one of Goldman's books at her bedside. Mother awakens to her passions and her strengths and is thus able to participate in the generative forces of history.

The little boy, one recalls, loves coincidences. The book is filled with them—chance meetings, unexpected incidents, accidental occurrences. Perhaps they are fitting for an age undergoing transformation, an age discovering relativity and the principle of uncertainty. As a musical meditation upon history, the novel shows two views of history in opposition. One is the view of the narrator, where history is seen as volatile and unpredictable. The other is the view held by J. P. Morgan, where history is repetition, reoccurrence. Morgan invests a small fortune into research that will support his theory of reincarnation. He believes that he and Ford are the reincarnations of the historical elite. When Morgan tries to interest Ford in his Egyptian projects, Ford shows that he holds, literally, a two-bit version of Morgan's ideas. Ford read about reincarnation in a pamphlet he bought from the Franklin Novelty Company. Ford is too busy duplicating machines to accompany Morgan to Egypt. Morgan continues his quest alone, hoping for a sign from the ancient gods. His night alone in a pyramid proves fruitless, except for the bedbugs. But such historical narcissism is doomed to failure, as is true of the ceaseless escapes of Houdini. No matter how hard he tries, Houdini cannot compete with the "real-world act." No matter how often he "defies death" he will still die—the earth will prove too heavy at last. Houdini is another frustrated quester, condemned by his art to imitate life. Only the little boy and the girl, in playing the serious "burial game" at the beach, are allowed a glimpse of rebirth. Obsessed with rebirth, Morgan, Ford, and Houdini see history almost wholly in terms of the self, an immature and infantile philosophy of history, one that is static and degenerate. Such a philosophy is a futile attempt to escape the moral responsibilities of finite life lived in historical process. But the Morgan–Ford–Houdini philosophy of escape endures, as the narrator says: "Today, nearly fifty years since his death, the audience for escapes is even larger."

Reality, history, will not be pinned down. History refuses to succumb to the impositions of the human ego. Dreiser turns his chair all night "seeking the proper alignment." Admiral Peary does not locate the exact spot of the North Pole: "On this watery planet the sliding sea refused to be fixed." Only a novel like a motion picture can hope to catch the experience of history. Such is *Ragtime*.

Reminiscent of Mark Twain's *Puddn'head Wilson*, the narrator recalls Freud's judgment of America after his visit: "America is a mistake, a gigantic mistake." There is much in the novel that might support such a view. But the "jolly relativity" of this carnivalesque novel may keep most readers from such a harsh verdict.

Note

21. Budick, *Fiction and Historical Consciousness*, p. 198.

FREDRIC JAMESON ON THE CULTURAL LOGIC OF LATE CAPITALISM

My point, however, is not some hypothesis as to the thematic coherence of this decentered narrative but rather just the opposite, namely, the way in which the kind of reading this novel imposes makes it virtually impossible for us to reach and thematize those official "subjects" which float above the text but cannot be integrated into our reading of the sentences. In that sense, the novel not only resists interpretation, it is organized systematically and formally to short-circuit an older type of social and historical interpretation which it perpetually holds out and withdraws. When we remember that the theoretical critique and repudiation of interpretation as such is a fundamental component of poststructuralist theory, it is difficult not to conclude that Doctorow has somehow deliberately built this very tension, this very contradiction, into the flow of his sentences.

The book is crowded with real historical figures—from Teddy Roosevelt to Emma Goldman, from Harry K. Thaw and Stanford White to J. Pierpont Morgan and Henry Ford, not to mention the more central role of Houdini—who interact with a fictive family, simply designated as Father, Mother, Older Brother, and so forth. All historical novels, beginning with those of Sir Walter Scott himself, no doubt in one way or another involve a mobilization of previous historical knowledge generally acquired through the schoolbook history manuals devised for whatever legitimizing purpose by this or that national tradition—thereafter instituting a narrative dialectic between what we already "know" about The Pretender, say, and what he is then seen to be concretely in the pages of the novel. But Doctorow's procedure seems much more extreme than this; and I would argue that the designation of both types of characters—historical names and capitalized family roles—operates powerfully and systematically to reify all these characters and to make it impossible for us to receive their representation without the prior interception of already acquired knowledge or doxa—something which lends the text an extraordinary sense of déjà vu and a peculiar familiarity one is tempted to associate with Freud's "return of the repressed" in "The Uncanny" rather than with any solid historiographic formation on the reader's part.

Meanwhile, the sentences in which all this is happening have their own specificity, allowing us more concretely to distinguish the moderns' elaboration of a personal style from this new kind of linguistic innovation, which is no longer personal at all but has its family kinship rather with what Barthes long ago called "white writing." In this particular novel, Doctorow has imposed upon himself a rigorous principle of selection in which only simple declarative sentences (predominantly mobilized by the verb "to be") are received. The effect is, however, not really one of the condescending simplification and symbolic carefulness of children's literature, but rather something more disturbing, the sense of some profound subterranean violence done to American English, which cannot, however, be detected empirically in any of the perfectly grammatical sentences with which this work is formed. Yet other more visible technical "innovations" may supply a clue to what is happening in the language of *Ragtime*: it is, for example, well known that the source of many of the characteristic effects of Camus's novel *The Stranger* can be traced back to that author's willful decision to substitute, throughout, the French tense of the *passé composé* for the other past tenses more normally employed in narration in that language.[11] I suggest that it is as if something of that sort were at work here: as though Doctorow had set out systematically to produce the effect or the equivalent, in his language, of a verbal past tense we do not possess in English, namely, the French preterite (or *passé simple*), whose "perfective" movement, as Émile Benveniste taught us, serves to separate events from the present of enunciation and to transform the stream of time and action into so many finished, complete, and isolated punctual event objects which find themselves sundered from any present situation (even that of the act of story telling or enunciation).

E.L. Doctorow is the epic poet of the disappearance of the American radical past, of the suppression of older traditions and moments of the American radical tradition: no one with left sympathies can read these splendid novels without a poignant distress that is an authentic way of confronting our own current political dilemmas in the present. What is culturally interesting, however, is that he has had to convey this great theme formally (since the waning of the content is very precisely his subject) and, more than that, has had to elaborate his work by way of that very cultural logic of the postmodern which is itself the mark and symptom of his dilemma. *Loon Lake* much more obviously deploys the strategies of the pastiche (most notably in its reinvention of Dos Passos); but Ragtime remains the most peculiar and stunning monument to the aesthetic situation engendered by the disappearance of the historical referent. This historical novel can no longer set out to represent the historical past; it can only "represent" our ideas and stereotypes about that past (which thereby at once becomes "pop history"). Cultural production is thereby driven back inside a mental space which is no longer that of the old monadic subject but rather that of some degraded collective "objective spirit": it can no longer gaze directly on some putative real world, at some reconstruction of a past history which was once itself a present; rather, as in Plato's cave, it must trace our mental images of that past upon its confining walls. If there is any realism left here, it is a "realism" that is meant to derive from the shock of grasping that confinement and of slowly becoming aware of a new and original historical situation in which we are condemned to seek History by way of our own pop images and simulacra of that history, which itself remains forever out of reach.

Note

11. Lean-Paul Sartre, "L'Etranger de Camus," in *Situations* II (Paris, Gallimard, 1948).

CHRISTOPHER D. MORRIS ON ILLUSIONS OF DEMYSTIFICATION

The undecidability of the narrator of *Ragtime* is the result of the generic names assigned to the primary family: Father, Mother, Mother's Younger Brother, and the little boy. The first three names appear to imply that the narrator is the little boy, the only child in the family. However, throughout the novel the little boy is referred to in the third, not the first person, as though he is not the narrator. The anonymous narrative voice of *Ragtime* appears to be the voice of an American writing in about the year 1975,[1] a person familiar with American cultural history and one who is given to both irony and rhetorical flourish.[2] With one exception, this narrative voice refers to itself as the editorial "we" when generalizing about history ("This was the time in our history"). The exception to this practice occurs near the end of the novel, when Father's death at sea, in the sinking of the *Lusitania*, is recounted: "Poor father, I see his final exploration. He arrives at the new place, his hair risen in astonishment, his mouth and eyes dumb. His toe scuffs a soft storm of sand, he kneels and his arms spread in pantomimic celebration, the immigrant, as in every moment of his life, arriving eternally on the shore of his Self" (368).

Some critics conclude, on the basis of this passage, that the narrator is the little boy grown up.[3] This inference can be supported by other internal evidence; for example, the narrator's knowledge of a visit from Houdini comes from "the family archives" (366). The full implications of this inference will be analyzed later; for now it is important to emphasize that the identification remains only inference: nowhere is the "I" explicitly identified as the little boy. Because the reader acquiesces to the convention of an anonymous narrator telling a story about characters known as Father, Mother, Mother's Younger Brother, and the little boy, the introduction of "I" instead of "we" does not remove the mystery. As other critics have maintained, the exceptional use of "I" can still refer to an anonymous narrator who names only an object of his narrative, not necessarily a relative.[4]

The ambiguity does not end there, for a third possibility is that the narrator is the little girl, Tateh's daughter Sha. Since the Yiddish words for father and mother are Tateh and Mameh, she occupies a position in the narrative equivalent to that of the little boy. If Sha is the narrator, then the scene in which she and Jung mutually experience a moment of recognition or telepathy (43) makes more comprehensible the narrator's otherwise inexplicable condemnation of Freud (39). Also, if Sha is the narrator, then the vivid detail in her recollection of a chance meeting with the little boy (104) becomes more comprehensible. There is yet a fourth possibility, that the editorial "we" refers to both Sha and the little boy speaking together. At the end of the novel, in Atlantic City, the two children are depicted as ideal, telepathic playmates, in the spirit of Goethe's "elective affinities" or Shelley's complementary lovers.[5] Although this possibility cannot be dismissed, it obviously creates new problems in examining the exceptional use of "I."

(...)

In order to read the novel, however, ultimate uncertainty cannot be tolerated; some attribution of a source to the words must be made. One act of naming that respects the enigma is to consider the narrator "double," that is simultaneously two different entities, a specific attribution and a separate, anonymous voice. In fact, such a practice could find some support in the novel's many images of duplication, especially in this description of the little boy's gazing at himself in the mirror: "He would gaze at himself until there were two selves facing one another, neither of which could claim to be the real one" (134). If no determinable source for this sentence (or for others in *Ragtime*) can be settled upon, then it embodies the very doubleness it describes. It suggests that an integral Cartesian self is not the originator of discourse but that, instead, a story can be told by two equally unreal entities. In this way, the novel's two unreal sources seem to demystify the illusion of a single consciousness as narrator.

Notes

1. The time of narration is established by the sentence "Today, nearly fifty years since [Houdini's] death, the audience for escapes is even larger" (8). Houdini died in 1926. The fact that the narrator is American is established by his many references to various times "in our history;" see for example pages 30, 103, 150, 177, 100, 230, 298, and 300.

2. In "Between Simultaneity and Sequence," DP, Richard King provides an excellent analysis of the narrator's shifting irony and tone. A typical sarcasm is the following: "There seemed to be quotas for death by starvation" (46). In the introduction to her *E.L. Doctorow: An Annotated Bibliography*, Michelle Tokarczyk argues that *Ragtime's* prose mocks that of history books (xv). The narrator's sometimes disconcerting rhetorical flourishes are especially evident in the beginning of new chapters, for example pages 109, 225, 279, 287.

3. In "The Stylistic Energy of E.L. Doctorow," EC, Arthur Saltzman writes that the narrator is "revealed at the conclusion of the novel as the Boy grown to adulthood" (95). In "Recomposing Time: Humboldt's Gift and *Ragtime*," *Denver Quarterly* 17 (1982): 16–31, Barbara L. Estrin contends, "We realize in the intrusion of the 'I' that the parent we had known all along as an archetype was a father to the writer" (19).

4. In "The Artist as Historian in the Novels of E.L. Doctorow," *Emporia State Research Studies* 29 (1980), Barbara Cooper argues that the narrator is anonymous and achieves aesthetic synthesis by adapting the techniques of photography (34). In "Between Simultaneity and Sequence," King argues that "the narrative voice of *Ragtime* is the voice of mass historical consciousness, but that voice is ironized by imaginary inverted commas standing, as it were, at either end of the narrative" (55). In "Doctorow's *Ragtime*: Narrative as Silhouette and Syncopation," *Dutch Quarterly Review of Anglo-American Letters* 11 (1981): 97–103, Susan Brienza also distinguishes the narrator from the little boy. Other readers acknowledge doubt about the identification. Mark Busby, in "E.L. Doctorow, *Ragtime*, and the Dialectics of Change," *Ball State University Forum* 26 (1980: 39–44, writes that the little boy is "possibly the narrator" (41). Bettina Friedl, in "The Stability of Images and the Instability of Things in E.L. Doctorow's Ragtime," DP, 91–104, says that the boy is "the central intelligence of at least parts of the novel" (101). In this section I use the words "narrator(s)" and "they" in the exploration of narratological uncertainty. Later in the chapter I revert to the words "narrator" and "he" where the possibility arises that the boy narrates. It is clear, however, that this usage is just as fictional as "narrator(s)."

5. The following sentence appears to endow the children with a unity so transcendent as to surpass physical separateness: "What bound them to each other was a fulfilled recognition which they lived and thought within so that their apprehension of each other could not be so distinct and separated as to include admiration for the other's fairness" (304). A statement of such extreme unity provides evidence for identifying the narrator as the two children speaking together. But this identification, like other nonanonymous ones, is vitiated by the possibility that the narrator may also be anonymous; see note 9, below. In addition to literary analogues in Goethe or Shelley, the relationship between the two children may evoke Jungian concepts. For example, Bettina Friedl finds in the play of the little boy and the little girl the articulation of Jung's anima or archetype (97).

BERNDT OSTENDORF
ON THE MUSICAL WORLD

What could E.L. Doctorow have had in mind when he chose *Ragtime* as the title of his best-selling novel of 1975? No more than a loose metaphor for an age if we go by the published literary criticism; for most of it focuses on narrative technique and the book's success or failure as a historical novel. It is time therefore to start reading the book completely, beginning with its title and the epigram by the black composer Scott Joplin.

Ragtime refers to a particular music, now considered timeless. But the term also identifies that era in the history of American music from 1896 to 1917, when Ragtime set a new agenda in popular music and ushered in a social revolution. While the first strains of this "novelty music" were heard as early as 1896, the ragtime "craze" began after the turn of the century. The time frame of Doctorow's novel extends from Stanford White's murder in 1906 to America's entry into World War I in 1916. The memory of the young boy, the principal narrator, reaches backward to 1902, when the house in New Rochelle was built, and forward to the marriage of Tateh and Mother in 1917, which happens to be the year of the Russian Revolution and of the first jazz recording. Doctorow's novel, then, covers the exact period when historical ragtime was a dominant style of American popular music.

Ragtime's historical significance and current meaning are not identical, and the novel's epistemology is inspired by this difference. Historical ragtime was pioneered by blacks and initially resisted by the Victorian musical establishment. But after 1900 ragtime lost its association with black musicians and became a "white" music by national adoption. Hence black sounds entered the American mainstream in whiteface, as it were. James T. Maher writes: "The straight line from plantation music to the earliest recorded jazz (1917) runs through ragtime: the impact of Negro syncopation is the major force in the Americanization of our popular music."[1] After 1917 ragtime was replaced by jazz and Tin Pan Alley and gradually lost its status as the queen of popular music.

The more recent renaissance of ragtime began in the early seventies with a best-selling classical record of Joplin rags, recorded by Joshua Rifkin, a classical pianist with degrees from Juilliard and Princeton. The rehabilitation of ragtime by the musical establishment would have pleased Joplin, who had always insisted that his compositions should be listed under classical music. But ragtime soon reasserted its crossover appeal and went slumming again.[2] The success of the musical score of the film *The Sting* restored ragtime to the popular market and expanded its contemporary audience considerably. However, it also helped to increase the distance from historical ragtime and to obscure further the role of its creators. The film score of Joplin's music was nominated for two Oscars, but the awards were given not to Joplin, but to Marvin Hamlish, who arranged the music for the film.[3]

If the ragtime renaissance of the seventies, which undoubtedly inspired the naming of the novel and helped to launch it to best-seller status, was a belated recognition of the music both in the classical and popular markets, it also constituted a subtle form of collective repression. A renaissance filters out the blood, sweat, and tears of the historical place and time that it evokes, while it foregrounds current, often nostalgic desire. This renaissance lifted ragtime out of its context and turned its history into metaphor or image (a key word in the novel). The historical music became the vehicle of a nostalgia for history with a set of associations quite different from the webs of significance in which the original producers and consumers were caught. The "rearrangement" of black-derived ragtime in our structure of feeling, credit for which goes to the rearranger, mirrors the previous, "mistaken" adoption of this black foundling and its successful career in white ragtime schools and publications. Understandably, the current nostalgia did not recognize that ragtime was in its time a revolutionary and an embattled black music and that one of its proud black creators died poor, alone, and maddened by the lack of public recognition. Indeed, the current "trivialized" recognition of ragtime as part of a throwaway musical culture may have shifted attention away from the story of ragtime which *Ragtime* tries to tell.

Doctorow articulates a justification for the "rediscovery" of ragtime and its age through the boy narrator, who not only "treasures anything discarded," but also is particularly interested in "meaning perceived through neglect."[4] This editorial aside invites us to read the novel as an attempt to reconstruct the conflict-laden musical universe at the time when ragtime entered into the mainstream of American music and to restore to consciousness what was repressed in the renaissance of ragtime. This reading is supported by a telling detail from Doctorow's biography which he elaborated on in his novel *World's Fair*. Doctorow's father ran a record store in Manhattan that served a mixed clientele of whites and blacks, and his uncle, a once famous jazz musician who had fallen on bad times, passed his knowledge of music history on to his nephew.

The "historical" novel *Ragtime*, then, is a form of biographical-anthropological fiction that apprehends and portrays, from the historical moment of the 1970s, the world of human desire and action of the turn of the century—history in the mode of participant observation over an interval of seventy years. This narrative stance, which deliberately merges past significance and present meaning, met with a mixed reaction from the novel's critics. Though the book was a popular success and received high praise, it was also called the most overrated novel of the year. Historians in particular found it antihistorical, anachronistic, frivolous, and irresponsible, a charge which, as this essay will argue, can only be upheld by readers deaf to the musical message.[5]

Notes

1. As quoted by Alec Wilder, *American Popular Song: The Great Innovators 1900–1950* (New York, 1972), 12.

2. Most of the credit for the academic rediscovery of ragtime must go to Rudi Blesh and Harriet Janis, *They All Played Ragtime* (New York, 1950), a groundbreaking study that has gone through many editions. Two recent publications stand out: Edward A. Berlin, *Ragtime: A Musical and Cultural History* (Berkeley, 1980) and John Edward Hasse, ed., *Ragtime: Its History, Composers, and Music* (New York, 1985).

3. Arnold Shaw, *Black Popular Music in America* (New York, 1986), 50.

4. E.L. Doctorow, *Ragtime* (New York, 1976), 131. All quotes are from this edition.

5. Richard Todd, "The-Most-Overrated-Book-of-the-Year-Award and other Literary Prizes," *Atlantic* (Jan. 1976): 95–96, and Cushing Strout, *The Veracious Imagination: Essays on American History, Literature, and*

Biography (Middletown, Conn., 1981) criticize the book for mixing history and fact. Barbara Foley, "From *U.S.A.* to *Ragtime*: Notes on the Forms of Historical Consciousness in Modern Fiction," in Richard Trenner, ed., *E.L. Doctorow: Essays & Conversations* (Princeton, N.J., 1983) draws unfavorable parallels to Dos Passos's work. See Paul Levine's *E.L. Doctorow* (London, 1985) for a more balanced assessment.

Works by E.L. Doctorow

Welcome to Hard Times, 1960.

Big as Life, 1966.

The Book of Daniel, 1971.

Ragtime, 1975.

Drinks Before Dinner, 1979.

Loon Lake, 1980.

E.L. Doctorow: Essays and Conversations, 1983.

Lives of the Poets: Six Stories and a Novella, 1984.

World's Fair, 1985.

Billy Bathgate, 1989.

Scenes and Sequences, 1989 (co-author with Eric Fischl).

Poets and Presidents, 1993.

Jack London, Hemingway, and the Constitution: Selected Essays, 1977–1992, 1993.

The Waterworks, 1994.

City of God, 2000.

Lamentation: 9/11, 2002.

Reporting the Universe, 2003.

Three Screenplays, 2003.

Annotated Bibliography

Barrett, Laura. "Compositions of Reality: Photography, History, and *Ragtime*." *Modern Fiction Studies* 46, no. 4 (Winter 2000): 801–824.

This essayist writes of the use of photography and history in *Ragtime*, and also describes the book in the context of the romance novel. While many critics have written of the work as cinematic, Barrett explains her view that it is actually "anti-cinematic."

Berryman, Charles. "*Ragtime* in Retrospect." *The South Atlantic Quarterly* 81, no. 1 (Winter 1982): 30–42.

Berryman reviews criticism of *Ragtime*, examining its initial, great positive reviews that were quickly followed by a torrent of negative ones. He points out some key aspects of the novel that some of the early reviewers overlooked and then focuses more closely on some of these. Berryman also takes an in-depth look at the narrator and also covers other items in the book such as mirror images and violence and rebirth.

Bloom, Harold, ed. *E.L. Doctorow's* Ragtime. Philadelphia: Chelsea House Publishers, 2002.

The essays in this volume have a range of original publication dates and cover an array of opinions and topics.

Budick, Emily Miller. "Seeking the Shores of Self: E.L. Doctorow's *Ragtime* and the Moral Fiction of History." *Fiction and Historical Consciousness*. New Haven and London: Yale University Press, 1989, 185–215.

This essay examines characters, their motivations, and the significance of the outcomes of their actions in detail. The author points to characters' flaws and their lack of understanding of themselves, and she explains that most are living in their own fantasies.

Emblidge, David. "Marching Backwards into the Future: Progress as Illusion in Doctorow's Novels." *Southwest Review* 62, no. 4 (Autumn 1977): 397–409.

Of all critics, Emblidge may hold the most pessimistic interpretation of Doctorow's vision in *Ragtime*. Emblidge sees this and other of Doctorow's works as showing an illusion, on the surface, of stability and refinement and a repetition underneath that is unchanging. History is far from a progression in this work; even though technological advances are rather rampant, human nature experiences little growth.

Foley, Barbara. "From *U.S.A.* to *Ragtime*: Notes on the Forms of Historical Consciousness in Modern Fiction." *American Literature* 50, no. 1 (March 1978): 85–105.

Foley compares *Ragtime* primarily to Dos Passos's *U.S.A.* She also explores the methods used in numerous works to document history and to interweave history and fiction.

Fowler, Douglas. "*Ragtime.*" In *Understanding E.L. Doctorow.* Columbia: University of South Carolina Press, 1992, 57–84.

Fowler provides some background on previous criticism and also goes through the book's plot, providing analysis along the way. Also provided is further commentary on Doctorow's use of coincidence and his overall style and message about America.

Gentry, Marshall Bruce. "*Ragtime* as Auto Biography." *Kansas Quarterly* 21, no. 4 (Fall 1989): 105–111.

This essayist focuses on the automobile to gain an understanding of *Ragtime*. He sees Doctorow's use of the auto as suggesting that man can be the individual he needs to be, despite society's pressures to conform. Gentry also looks at the issues of duplicability and individuality primarily in terms of the Little Boy.

Hague, Angela. "*Ragtime* and the Movies." *North Dakota Quarterly* 50, no. 3 (Summer 1982): 101–112.

This essay focuses solely on photography and film as thematic elements making statements about reality, time, change, and duplicability. Also discussed is film's appeal to the working class and the "new aesthetic" in American art.

Harpham, Geoffrey Galt. "E.L. Doctorow and the Technology of Narrative." *PMLA* 100, no. 1 (January 1985): 81–95.

This critic sees *Ragtime* as focusing on transformation, human identity, the individual's relationship to society, and technology. In the work, he points out, those characters that are happy at the end are those who recognized that their selves must change and who are able to manage in a volatile world.

Jameson, Fredric. "The Cultural Logic of Late Capitalism." *Postmodernism, or, The Cultural Logic of Late Capitalism.* Durham: Duke University Press, 1991, 1–54.

Doctorow's use of language is pondered in this essay— namely his use of tense and simple declarative sentences, which this essayist sees as indicating a destruction of the English language itself and an aid to show Doctorow's point that the past is separated from the present. He calls Doctorow "the epic poet of the disappearance of the American radical past."

Jones, Phyllis M. "*Ragtime*: Feminist, Socialist and Black Perspectives on the Self-Made Man." *Journal of American Culture* 2 (Spring 1979): 17–28.

This is one of the few essays specifically devoted to *Ragtime* that takes a feminist perspective. Jones looks at Doctorow's three male heads of households as self-made men. She argues that Doctorow includes Emma Goldman in the book to ridicule America for revering the self-starter.

Karl, Frederick. "More Mid-1970s: Doctorow, Sukenick, Theroux." *American Fictions, 1940–1980.* New York: Harper & Row, 1983, 514–520.

Karl looks at *Ragtime* as a circus, with a main narrative and multiple sideshows. He sees the book as Doctorow's response to the sixties and as assimilating techniques of music, television, film, and stage. At the same time, Karl calls the novel "an expert job," and examines Doctorow's perspective on history and the individual.

Lukacs, John. "Doctorowulitzer or History in Ragtime." *Salmagundi* 31–32 (Fall 1975–Winter 1976): 285–295.

The critic points out what he sees as numerous flaws in the text. For example, he is diappointed by the fact that the real people in the book do things they would not do in the real world. Also, he points to Doctorow's over-attentiveness to items of the time. He discusses the pictorial, rather than literary, imagination in the work.

Morris, Christopher D. "Illusions of Demystification in *Ragtime*." *Models of Misrepresentation: On the Fiction of E.L. Doctorow*. Jackson and London: University Press of Mississippi, 1991, 98–114.

While many have puzzled or made assumptions about who the narrator is in *Ragtime*, Morris looks at the issue in more detail and from numerous vantages. He also examines characters' actions, beliefs, and their consequences, and gives his perception of the Little Boy that is different from most others. He points to numerous illusions Doctorow incorporates in the work as well.

Neumeyer, Peter F. "E.L. Doctorow, Kleist, and the Ascendancy of Things." *CEA Critic* 39, no. 4 (May 1977): 17–21.

This is one of the earliest essays comparing Coalhouse Walker Jr. to his nineteenth-century prototype, Heinrich von Kleist's Michael Kohlhaas. Neumeyer speaks not just of the characters' similarities but also of *Ragtime* as moving in a new direction, calling it "the anti-person book," since it focuses not on the hero but on things.

Parks, John G. "Compositions of Dissatisfaction: *Ragtime*." *E.L. Doctorow*. New York: Continuum Publishing, 1991, 56–70.

This essayist examines Doctorow's perspective on history, as represented in the Little Boy's perspective that history is constantly changing and in Morgan's perspective that it is constantly repeating. Parks observes characters' infantile views and sees many characters as concerned almost totally with the self and with escape from "the moral responsibility of finite life lived in historical process."

Raban, Jonathan. "Easy Virtue." *Encounter* 46, no. 2 (February 1976): 71–4.

One of the earliest of negative commentators, Raban disparages Doctorow for his poor job of combining journalism, history, and fiction in *Ragtime*. The book's peaks are superficial, in his view. Its real-life people are lacking, and overall the work falls apart when examined on its literary merit.

Trenner, Richard, ed. *E.L. Doctorow: Essays and Conversations.* Princeton: Ontario Review Press, 1983.

This is one of the few anthologies of Doctorow criticism. While Doctorow has given numerous interviews, he still has warned that it is better to read his books than the interviews. Nevertheless, this text provides not just interviews but other work that provides insight into the author's writing and ideas.

Williams, John. "*Ragtime* as Historical Novel, 1977–85." In *Fiction as False Document: The Reception of E.L. Doctorow in the Postmodern Age.* Columbia, S.C: Camden House, 1996, 37–59.

Williams provides an in-depth look at some of the key criticism on *Ragtime* that was published between 1977 and 1985. He categorizes critics based on their approaches and shows how their perceptions of the historical novel changed over time.

Contributors

Harold Bloom is Sterling Professor of the Humanities at Yale University. He is the author of over 20 books, including *Shelley's Mythmaking* (1959), *The Visionary Company* (1961), *Blake's Apocalypse* (1963), *Yeats* (1970), *A Map of Misreading* (1975), *Kabbalah and Criticism* (1975), *Agon: Toward a Theory of Revisionism* (1982), *The American Religion* (1992), *The Western Canon* (1994), and *Omens of Millennium: The Gnosis of Angels, Dreams, and Resurrection* (1996). *The Anxiety of Influence* (1973) sets forth Professor Bloom's provocative theory of the literary relationships between the great writers and their predecessors. His most recent books include *Shakespeare: The Invention of the Human* (1998), a 1998 National Book Award finalist, *How to Read and Why* (2000), *Genius: A Mosaic of One Hundred Exemplary Creative Minds* (2002), and *Hamlet: Poem Unlimited* (2003). In 1999, Professor Bloom received the prestigious American Academy of Arts and Letters Gold Medal for Criticism, and in 2002 he received the Catalonia International Prize.

Pamela Loos has written and/or researched more than 35 books of literary criticism, covering authors ranging from Goethe to Cormac McCarthy. She is the project editor of *Women Memoirists, Vol. II*.

Peter F. Neumeyer is the editor of *Twentieth Century Interpretations of The Castle*. He is also a translator.

Barbara Foley is the author of *Radical Representations: Politics & Form in U.S. Proletarian Fiction, 1929–1941*. She is also the co-author of numerous educational books on English and grammar. She has taught at Rutgers University in Newark.

Frederick R. Karl teaches English at New York University. He is the author of *The Contemporary English Novel, An Age of*

Fiction: The Nineteenth Century British Novel, and several other titles. He is also the editor or co-editor of numerous books.

Geoffrey Galt Harpham teaches at Tulane University. He has published *One of Us: The Mastery of Joseph Conrad* and other titles.

Emily Miller Budick has published *American Romance Fiction: The Nineteenth Century* and *Engendering Romance: Women Writers and the Hawthorne Tradition, 1850–1990.*

Marshall Bruce Gentry teaches at the University of Indianapolis. He is the author of *Flannery O'Connor's Religion of the Grotesque* and the joint editor of other titles.

Cushing Strout is Ernest I. White Professor of American Studies and Humane Letters, Emeritus at Cornell University. He is the author of *The American Image of the Old World.*

John G. Parks teaches English at Miami University. He has published *American Short Stories since 1945.*

Fredric Jameson is a Professor at Duke University and is the author of numerous books, including *The Political Unconscious: Narrative as a Socially Symbolic Act.*

Christopher D. Morris is the editor of *Conversations with E.L. Doctorow,* the author of several books, and the editor or joint editor of many others.

Berndt Ostendorf has been a Professor of American Studies at Amerika Institut München. He writes on music and ethnicity in America.

Acknowledgments

"E.L. Doctorow, Kleist, and the Ascendancy of Things" by Peter F. Neumeyer. From *The CEA Critic* 39, no. 4 (May 1977): 18–20, 21. ©1977 by the College English Association, Inc. Reprinted by permission.

"From *U.S.A.* to *Ragtime*: Notes on the Forms of Historical Consciousness in Modern Fiction" by Barbara Foley. From *American Literature* 50, no. 1 (March 1978): 102–104. ©1978 by Duke University Press. Reprinted by permission.

"More Mid-1970s: Doctorow, Sukenick, Theroux" by Frederick R. Karl. *From American Fictions, 1940/1980*: 514–15. ©1983 by Frederick R. Karl. Reprinted by permission.

"E.L. Doctorow and the Technology of Narrative" by Geoffrey Galt Harpham. From *PMLA* 100, no. 1 (January 1985): 89–90. ©1985 by The Modern Language Association of America. Reprinted by permission.

"Seeking the Shores of Self: E.L. Doctorow's *Ragtime* and the Moral Fiction of History," by Emily Miller Budick. From *Fiction and Historical Consciousness: 202–204*. ©1989 by Yale University. Reprinted by permission.

"*Ragtime* as Auto Biography" by Marshall Bruce Gentry. From *Kansas Quarterly* 21, no. 4 (Fall 1989): 108–110. ©1990 by the *Kansas Quarterly*. Reprinted by permission.

"Twain, Doctorow, and the Anachronistic Adventures of the Arms Mechanic and the Jazz Pianist" by Cushing Strout. From *Making American Tradition*: 118, 121–23. ©1990 by Cushing Strout. Reprinted by permission of Rutgers University Press.

Index